ECUMENISM

PRESENT REALITIES
AND
FUTURE PROSPECTS

ECUMENISM

PRESENT REALITIES
AND
FUTURE PROSPECTS

*Papers Read at the
Tantur Ecumenical Center,
Jerusalem, 1997*

∞

Edited by
LAWRENCE S. CUNNINGHAM

University of Notre Dame Press
Notre Dame, Indiana

Library of Congress Cataloging-in-Publication Data

Ecumenism : present realities and future prospects / edited by
    Lawrence S. Cunningham.
        p.   cm.
    "Papers read at the Tantur Ecumenical Center, Jerusalem, 1997."
    Includes bibliographical references.
    ISBN 0-268-02752-8 (hardcover : alk. paper)
    1. Tantur Ecumenical Center (Jerusalem)—Congresses.
    2. Ecumenical movement—Congresses.   I. Cunningham, Lawrence.
    II. Tantur Ecumenical Center (Jerusalem)
    BX6.T36E28   1998
    280'.042—dc21   98-34306

Contents

Preface   vii
Edward A. Malloy, C.S.C.

Introduction   ix
Lawrence S. Cunningham

Contributors   xi

ONE   The Traditions That Divide, the Tradition
That Unites   1
Jaroslav Pelikan

TWO   The Churches in the Middle East   25
Frans Bouwen

THREE   The Churches in Jerusalem   37
Frans Bouwen

FOUR   Ecumenical Education and Formation:
An Urgent Need for Further Progress in Ecumenical
and Interfaith Relations   51
Cardinal Edward Idris Cassidy

FIVE   The Present Status of the Ecumenical Movement   61
Anna-Marie Aagaard

SIX   Three Morning Biblical Meditations   79
Peter Coleman

SEVEN   The Rift That Binds: Hermeneutical Approaches
to the Jewish-Christian Relationship   95
Michael A. Signer

EIGHT   The Unity We Still Seek:
             An Eastern Orthodox Perspective   117
                Thomas Hopko

NINE   Towards an Ecumenical Ecclesiology
             of Communion   133
                Jean M. R. Tillard, O.P.

TEN   The Reception Process: The Challenge at
             the Threshold of a New Phase of the
             Ecumenical Movement   149
                Hermann J. Pottmeyer

ELEVEN   Power and Authority in Ecumenical Theology   169
                Stephen Sykes

Preface

Twenty-five years ago Pope Paul VI asked Father Theodore Hesburgh, C.S.C., a close personal friend and then president of the University of Notre Dame, to establish and build an ecumenical center in Jerusalem for the study of theology. This project became a personal one for Father Hesburgh. A beautiful site in the West Bank of the Jordan River, on a hill called "Tantur," was secured by the Holy See. The location was on the road between Bethlehem and Jerusalem.

The description of this site contains within itself so much of the monotheistic religions and so many of the exciting challenges ecumenical and interreligious efforts encompass.

While the land on which Tantur is located had been Jordanian, part of the occupied West Bank, and, ultimately, an annexed portion of the city of Jerusalem itself, the goals of the foundation have remained a simple attempt to witness to the holiness of the land and of the peoples, and to be a place where all who worship the One True God can feel welcome.

A significant benefaction of I. A. O'Shaughnessy made it possible for the magnificent building which now stands atop Tantur to be constructed.

The generous support of the University of Notre Dame, the British Trust, the French Association, and countless benefactors, many of whom profited personally from time spent on this holy hill, have enabled the Institute to come to be, to survive, and even to thrive.

As we found ourselves on the threshold of celebrating the twenty-fifth annversary of the realization of the dream of Pope Paul VI for a place open to those who seek the Lord with sincere hearts, it was only fitting to mark the occasion with a conference on the current state of ecumenism. These proceedings are dedicated to Father Theodore Hesburgh, C.S.C., and Bishop Pierre Duprey, M.Afr., and to the memory of Canon Charles Moeller, the three who made this place a reality.

May what has been accomplished in this special place up until now be only a foretaste of what might come to those who place their trust in the Lord of Life.

Edward A. Malloy, C.S.C.
President
University of Notre Dame
Tantur—Jerusalem
August 15, 1997

Introduction

At a meeting of the advisory board of the Tantur Center in the city of Exeter, England, it was decided that there should be a conference at Tantur in 1997 to "take the pulse" of ecumenical relationships and to make some realistic judgments about future prospects for greater Christian unity. It was a felicitious notion for a number of reasons. Tantur would celebrate, in that year, its twenty-fifth anniversary and, happily, the conference would be held in the same month (May) that Theodore Hesburgh, C.S.C., would celebrate his eightieth birthday. Father Hesburgh along with Bishop Pierre Duprey and the late Canon Charles Moeller were the ones who made Pope Paul VI's dream of an ecumenical research center in Jerusalem a reality.

Members of the board gave the conference organizer some very helpful suggestions. Bishop Peter Coleman, who hosted us at Exeter, offered to add a spiritual dimension to our gathering by providing some meditations on the psalms. Father Thomas Stransky, who as rector at Tantur facilitated the conference, insisted that we not neglect the Jerusalem Church, and that suggestion has seen its fruition in the contributions of Frans Bouwen. Remi Hoeckman, O.P., wisely reminded us that one cannot speak of ecumenism today without attention to the Jewish roots of Christianity, which encouraged us to invite Michael Signer to speak. The other speakers bring a wide acquaintance with, and a profound passion for, religious unity. Professor Pelikan was deeply involved as a commentator on the proceedings of the Second Vatican Council, while Jean-Marie Tillard, Anna-Marie Aagaard, Stephen Sykes, Thomas Hopko, and Hermann Pottmeyer all bring wide ecumenical experience, a high theological culture, and intellectual honesty to their work. Cardinal Edward Cassidy, who carries the papal portfolio for ecumenical and interreligious matters, graced us with his presence.

The days of the conference were full. We had papers spaced out enough so that there was time for dialogue and vigorous exchange. We were pleased with the participation of people who came from abroad for the proceedings as well as large representations from the local Orthodox, Roman Catholic, Protestant, and Eastern Churches, who added so much to our discussions.

In the midst of all our theological discussions we also found time to fete Father Hesburgh on his birthday—an event which included a visit by retired Jerusalem mayor Teddy Kollek as well as hierarchs, monastics, clergy, and members of the diplomatic corps. A surprise visit by the Notre Dame Glee Club, which was then touring in Israel, added a festive note to our celebration, a celebration made all the more wonderful due to the hospitality of the Tantur community.

The papers read at the Tantur Conference are all characterized by their sobriety in judging the ecumenical status quo and the vigor of their hopes for the future. None reflect the flushed enthusiasm that characterized the end of the council but neither do they despair of that hope which finds itself embedded in the prayer of Jesus which Pope John Paul II took as the title of his recent encyclical on ecumenism: *Ut Omnes Unum Sint.*

The sense of community engendered during our days together at Tantur is hard to detect through the more austere medium of scholarly papers. We enjoyed the companionship of a delegation of members from the French Association thanks to the efforts of Nicholas and Veronique Lossky (Father Tillard's paper was given in French; its translation is the work of Donata Coleman, who was a long time translator for the World Council of Churches). We had with us former resident scholars sponsored by the British Trust, such as Judith Lieu, as well as former students also courtesy of the British Trust. The intermingling, conversation, and worship which was a part of this conference was ample enough proof of the value of this place called Tantur. Our common prayer is that it will continue to be so in the future as we move towards the new millenium.

These papers are the fruit of the labors at Tantur and a pledge for the future of religious unity. They are published in that spirit.

Lawrence S. Cunningham
The University of Notre Dame
October 4, 1997—Feast of St. Francis of Assisi

Contributors

Anna-Marie Aagaard is president of the World Council of Churches (University of Aarhus, Denmark).

Frans Bouwen is rector of Saint Anne's Church (Jerusalem).

Cardinal Edward Idris Cassidy is president of the Pontifical Council of Christian Unity (Vatican City).

Peter Coleman is retired bishop of Credition (England).

Lawrence S. Cunningham is Professor of Theology at the University of Notre Dame (USA).

Thomas Hopko is rector of St. Vladimir's Orthodox Seminary (USA).

Edward A. Malloy, C.S.C., is president of the University of Notre Dame (USA).

Jaroslav Pelikan is Sterling Professor Emeritus of History at Yale University (USA).

Hermann Pottmeyer is Professor of Fundamental Theology at the Ruhr University, Bochum (Germany).

Michael Signer is Abrams Professor of Jewish Studies at the University of Notre Dame (USA).

Stephen Sykes is bishop of Ely (England).

Jean-Marie Tillard, O.P., is vice president of the WCC Faith and Order Commission (Canada).

ONE

The Traditions That Divide, the Tradition That Unites

Jaroslav Pelikan

∞

The Ecumenical Center at Tantur stands as a living monument to the historic meeting on 5–6 January 1964 at the Mount of Olives between His Holiness Pope Paul VI and His All-Holiness Patriarch Athenagoras I, thus between the patriarch of Old Rome and the patriarch of New Rome. Lest that event of a third of a century ago become no more than one of those happenings that are remembered fondly but that do not really change anything, the Center at Tantur was founded exactly a fourth of a century ago, and in Jerusalem, because, as it was said in the founding document, "there Christ founded in the Spirit the one undivided church, and today Christians of all communions, one yet sadly divided, find other 'peoples of the Book,' Jews and Muslims."[1] Since that time Tantur has proved to be a blessing to the life of all the churches, a stimulus to creative scholarship, and a model of how at one and the same time to carry on fraternal disagreement and achieve fraternal agreement, thus how to obey the apostolic imperative of "speaking the truth in love" (Eph. 4:15)—neither truth without love nor love without truth.

"The Traditions That Divide, the Tradition That Unites" is a historical and theological issue, or set of issues, with far-reaching consequences for the many-faceted challenges of ecumenism, and therefore for the mission of this pioneering center. Here in Israel, the obvious form of that challenge would be to address the first schism in Christian history, the alienation of the Church from the People of Israel its mother, an alienation whose implications did not become fully visible in all their enormity until the twentieth century. Also close at hand all around us as an illustration both of the traditions that divide and of the Tradition that unites are the divisions between the three monotheisms of the Book, each of which has been fragmented by its history and all of which name Abraham as their father and are simultaneously united in him but separated through him. The land of the Bible is, moreover, a particularly poignant reminder that it has been over the Bible, which is in a special sense the Tradition that unites, that Protestantism and Roman Catholicism have been divided—over its authority in relation to Tradition and the Church, over its interpretation at many key places, even over the very question of the scope of its canon. Any of these would be a fitting topic for the consideration of my assigned theme, and all of them together would make a book, indeed a book of many volumes.

The epoch-making encounter commemorated by this center as well as the growing concentration of my own scholarly work during these same twenty-five years on the history of Eastern Christianity, Byzantine and Slavic, points me in the direction of the relation between Eastern and Western Christendom as the prime example both of traditions that divide and of the Tradition that unites, not only in its own right as an issue that has sometimes seemed to be dormant but has come to life especially in the thirty-three years since that long-delayed fraternal embrace on the Mount of Olives, but also as the one separation whose tragic ironies highlight, more dramatically than any other, the profound ambiguities of my assigned theme, "The Traditions That Divide, the Tradition That Unites."[2]

It is supremely ironic that the schism between the Roman Catholic West and the Orthodox East rests upon an enormous body of shared Tradition that unites and that is not, moreover, shared in the same way or to the same degree by any of the other Christian divisions: the seven indisputably ecumenical councils of Nicaea (325), Constantinople I (381), Ephesus (431), Chalcedon (451), Constantinople II (553), Constantinople III (680–781), and Nicaea II (783), with all their decrees prescribing normative doctrine and proper Christian practice; the fundamental outlines of sacramental worship and devotion; the structure of hierarchical authority in priesthood, episcopacy, and patriarchate; the thousands and thousands of pages of the writings of the orthodox Greek and Latin fathers, who are accepted as authoritative throughout both communities; the heritages of monastic and of mystical spirituality created by devoted women and men in every time and every place; and the veneration of the Blessed Virgin Mary and the other saints. Therefore, when, for example, the second and third generations of Protestant Reformers sought to establish common ground with Constantinople on the basis of their also being separated from the see of Rome, even translating the Augsburg Confession into Greek, they were rebuffed, politely but firmly, on the basis of the presence and even greater importance in the East of some of the very elements, such as the prominence of the Theotokos, against which they were protesting in the Latin West.[3]

Then what could have gone so tragically wrong? How and why did the traditions that divided East from West manage to prevail so successfully over the Tradition that united East with West during the first eight centuries or so and that still unites them today even across the great divide? Although it may come as a surprise to those who have not studied the problem except as it appears in the standard textbooks and encyclopedias, it is noteworthy that the very date of the schism is a problem, not alone for canon law, but especially for any historiography that penetrates beneath the surface. At the risk of imposing an artificial schematism on intractable historical forces, I propose to employ that problem of date as a heuristic device for my review and perhaps as a clue to the *status quo ante bellum* of the undivided Church. I shall examine, in analytic vignettes rather than connected narratives, the implications of six possible dates for the triumph of the traditions that divide over the Tradition that unites, considering them not in chronological order but from the most commonly cited to one that is not cited but almost could be, namely, 1054; 867; 1204; 800; 1576; and 1341–1368. Each date involves a different diagnosis of the traditions that divide and a different paradigm of the Tradition that unites. Taken together, they become a comprehensive if not exhaustive catalog of "The Traditions That Divide, the Tradition That Unites."

1054: Jurisdictional Unity

If jurisdictional unity is constitutive of the Tradition that unites and if its violation unleashes the traditions that divide, then the mutual excommunications of 1054 mark the correct date for the schism.

On 16 July 1054, "shaking the dust from their feet, [the pope's legates] deposited on the altar of St. Sophia a direful anathema. . . . The Greeks have never recanted their errors; the popes have never repealed their sentence; and from this thunderbolt we may date the consummation of the schism."[4] Such is the account of the schism in the most influential work of history ever written in the English language, Edward Gibbon's *History of the Decline and Fall of the Roman Empire*. One Eastern Orthodox reference work, that of Karmirēs, which perhaps comes nearest to being an authoritative compilation of Eastern Orthodox creeds and confessions of faith, likewise interprets the events of 1054 as decisive, reprinting the Epistle of Michael I Cerularius to Peter of Antioch as the key document for the East.[5] On the Latin side, Cardinal Humbert in his writ of excommunication declared: "Let Michael Cerularius, the novice and falsely so-called patriarch [and his associates] . . . be anathema, with all heretics, indeed with the devil and his angels, unless by some chance they come to their senses. Amen, Amen, Amen."[6]

Thus 1054 has become the standard date in the textbooks.[7] But the revisionist historiography of the mid-twentieth century has convincingly documented the inadequacy of this definition of the schism on several counts, two of which are closely connected and are deserving of mention here.[8] First, a close reading of the texts of these "thunderbolts" makes it clear that the object of the excommunicating condemnation on either side was not the patriarchal see of Old Rome or of New Rome as such, much less all of Western or Eastern Christendom. The anathemas condemn Michael Cerularius or Humbert of Silva Candida—as more than isolated individuals, to be sure, but certainly as less than their entire churches.[9] Secondly, any answer to the question of how divided the two parts of Christendom actually were after 1054 must take into account the continuing practices of intercommunion at many places and the prayers "for all thy people [*peri pantos tou laou sou*]" at the same altar of Hagia Sophia where the excommunication had been deposited, which still listed on the official diptychs among this "people of God" the not-quite-separated sister church of the Latin obedience.[10]

Even after that important revision, it needs to be added, however, that the distinction with which I have been working here between jurisdictional unity and the Tradition that unites is in some highly significant respects flawed and misleading; for both East and West came to regard what is anachronistically called jurisdictional unity as a doctrinal question, and one on which there was fundamental difference between them. Western scholars like Francis Dvornik and Eastern scholars like John Meyendorff have demonstrated beyond contradiction that except for occasional aberrations, such as a later treatise falsely attributed to Patriarch Photius,[11] Eastern teachers were agreed on the primacy of Peter as *prōtothrōnos* among the apostles, and therefore the primacy of the see of Peter among apostolic sees, even though his brother and fellow apostle Andrew, as *prōtoklētos,* did occupy his own special place.[12] But from this shared assumption, this Tradition that united them, they drew opposing conclusions, traditions that divided them. The conventional, if perhaps simplistic, way of putting it is that for Eastern teaching, Peter, as well as each successor to the throne of Peter in Rome, was not a monarch but *primus inter pares,* the other *pares* being Constantinople, Alexandria, Antioch, and Jerusalem: the principle of pentarchy as distinct from monarchy. Even the authority of all five apostolic patriarchates put together, moreover, did not belong on the same level as conciliar authority, specifically the authority of the first seven ecumenical councils, all of them held in the East. During the Middle Ages, by contrast, Western theory about jurisdictional unity gradually evolved into a doctrine of monarchy that elevated the Patriarch of Rome over the other four patriarchs, and eventually over the authority of the councils,[13] with the crisis coming at the reform councils of the fifteenth century. By 1054 that evolution had moved a long way in this direction, so that if the mutual excommunications are seen not as isolated acts but as a sign of fundamental change and fundamental difference, the date retains (or regains) some degree of plausibility.

867: Unity in Dogma, Pluralism in Theologies

If the Tradition that unites is expressed or even guaranteed by a unity in dogma, and if lack of acquaintance with its full range is responsible for the rise of a pluralism in theologies that allows particular theologumena to become traditions that divide, then the "Photian schism" and the controversies over the Filioque identify 867 or some date near that as a possible candidate for the dubious honor of being the date of the divorce.

It becomes painfully evident in one Eastern Orthodox document after another—to cite one modern example, the "Encyclical Against the Latin Innovations" issued by the Synod of Constantinople in 1838, which still lists it first among the Western *kainotomiai* to be condemned[14]—that on no point of doctrine, neither papal primacy nor original sin nor purgatory nor salvation as deification-*theōsis*, has the separation been as theologically momentous as on the Trinity, as that difference is expressed in the Western addition to the Nicene Creed, "the faith of the 318 fathers," when it says that the Holy Spirit "proceeds from the Father and the Son [*ex Patre Filioque procedit*]"; and no Western theologian has been as momentous in creating that difference as Augustine.[15] At the risk of oversimplifying a complex issue on which many thinkers in East and West have written at great length—let me identify just one central dogmatic and exegetical issue here for which a better Western knowledge of the Tradition that unites might have forestalled traditions that divide. In John 15:26 Christ says: "When the Counselor comes, whom I shall send to you from the Father [*hon egō pempsō hymin para tou patros*], even the Spirit of truth who proceeds from the Father [*ho para tou patros ekporeuetai*], he will bear witness to me."

What is the relation between the "sending [Greek *pempsis*, Latin *missio*]" of the Spirit referred to in the first relative clause and the "proceeding [Greek *ekporeusis*, Latin *processio*]" of the Spirit in the second?

The Greek church fathers and, following them, the theologians of Byzantium commonly answered that question by applying to it one of their most fundamental distinctions, that between the relation of Father, Son, and Holy Spirit (which they called theology [*theologia*] and the relation of God to creation and history which they called economy [*oikonomia*]): the proceeding of the Holy Spirit belongs to theology, thus to eternity, and is, as this verse says—and as the original text of the Creed confirms—from the Father as the single *archē;* the sending of the Holy Spirit belongs to economy, thus to time and history, and is from both the Father and the Son, so that the Gospel can say here that the Son sends the Spirit from the Father and in the preceding chapter (John 14:26) that the Father sends the Spirit in the Son's name. Although the Greek fathers are not entirely consistent in this regard[16] and although, conversely, there are passages in Augustine and other Latins where that distinction does appear,[17] the formula of Pope Saint Gregory the Great, "being sent [*missio*] is the very procession [*processio*] by which [the Holy Spirit] proceeds from the Father and from the Son,"[18] epitomized the Western position, for which therefore the unilateral Western alteration of the text of the Creed was a logical conclusion.

Underlying this Western development of a tradition that divides was lack of acquaintance with the full range of the Tradition that unites, a problem exacerbated by ignorance of language. For in a circumstance starkly noted by Augustine's most illustrious present-day biographer, Peter Brown,

> [As a schoolboy] Augustine found that Greek bored him to distraction at just the same time as he had begun to "revel" in the Latin Classics. Augustine's failure to learn Greek was a momentous casualty of the Late Roman educational system: he will become the only Latin philosopher in antiquity to be virtually ignorant of Greek. . . . Greek culture did not just drain away of its own accord from Augustine's Africa. The one man who might have brought it alive there, replaced it by constantly giving and creating.[19]

If, as Brown suggests, that inability to read Greek had far-reaching philosophical implications, making Augustine dependent for example on Cicero's translation of Plato's *Timaeus*, the dogmatic implications of his inability to read Greek proved to be even more calamitous and downright tragic. At several crucial points in *De Trinitate* Augustine acknowledged and demonstrated that he was simply ignorant—*nescio* is his own Latin word—of the works of the Greek Trinitarian theologians who had immediately preceded him, above all the Cappadocians, and therefore that he was not able to operate with the Greek definitions and distinctions of their writings.[20] What he could have derived from this Tradition that unites, he, in Peter Brown's words, "replaced by constantly giving and creating," in the dazzling theological tour de force that he brought off in the second half of *De Trinitate*—one of the true masterpieces in the history of Christian speculation. But our admiration for that speculative tour de force must be tempered by the sobering awareness of the consequences of the Augustinian *nescio* for the separation between East and West.

Was Augustine's formulation of the Filioque a Trinitarian heresy or a permissible theologoumenon?[21] In an effort to turn this tradition that divides into a Tradition that could unite, John Henry Newman, whose knowledge of the fourth-century Greek fathers had few rivals at the middle of the nineteenth century, nevertheless felt able to say about the Filioque: "The doctrine of the Double Procession was no Catholic dogma in the first ages, though it was more or less clearly stated by individual Fathers; yet if it is now to be received, as surely it must be, as part of the Creed, *it was really held everywhere from the beginning,* and therefore, in a measure, held as a mere religious impression, and perhaps an unconscious one"; Owen Chadwick has called this "one of those frustrating passages which from time to time baffle and trouble every reader of Newman," because of the relation between Newman the theologian and Newman the historian.[22]

The "Photian schism," as articulated by the Council of Constantinople in 867, is sometimes said to represent the first identification of Filioque as divisive. But as Francis Dvornik has said, the Council of Constantinople in 867 was an event about which "little of what occurred there has reached us"; nevertheless, it does seem sure not only that "Pope Nicholas was judged and condemned," but also "that such accounts of the Council as have come down to us nowhere mention any condemnation of the Western Church on the grounds of any false doctrine she might have been teaching."[23] At issue in Eastern objections to the Filioque was, alongside the substantive dogmatic issue, the supposedly unchangeable status of "the *ekthesis* of the 318 fathers." This is commonly called the Nicene Creed, as though it were the text adopted in 325 at the Council of Nicaea. As everyone knows (or should know by now), what Nicaea adopted, Constantine enforced, and Athanasius defended was in fact a creed that differs significantly from the one that eventually bore the name of the council. It was not Nicaea in 325, but Constantinople in 381, that promulgated our "Nicene Creed." To recover this Niceno-Constantinopolitan Creed, moreover, we are obliged to turn not even to the decrees of 381 as such, which are fragmentary, but to the more amply preserved and transmitted decrees of the Fourth Ecumenical Council, the Council of Chalcedon of 451.[24] Taking it at face value, we identify this as the Creed of 381, but in traditional usage it is identified as though it were the Creed of 325. Which raises the troubling question of just how unchangeable a creed may be regarded as being if it could be revised as it was from 325 to 381, and the further question of whether the addition of the Filioque was, speaking now formally and not dogmatically, a more drastic change in the text of the unchangeable creed than were all the changes that we now attribute to the Council of Constantinople. Also deserving of attention are the attitudes of the papacy toward the Filioque, beginning with an initial reluctance and only much later coming to an official acceptance, as subsequent considerations of it likewise show.[25]

1204: Fraternity, if not Liberty or Equality

If the bond of an enduring fraternity stands as a Tradition that unites even despite the prevalence of these other traditions that divide, the violation of that fraternal bond by the Western sack of Constantinople and by attendant actions such as the founding of the Latin patriarchate suggests 1204 as the date of the estrangement.

Whatever may be the ecclesiastical justification for regarding the schism of Michael Cerularius in 1054 as the decisive action, or the dogmatic justification for defining the Filioque and therefore perhaps the council of 867 as the decisive issue, the event that looms above all others in Eastern consciousness to the present day is the sack of previously impregnable Constantinople by Western Crusaders in 1204 and attendant action such as the founding of the Latin patriarchate.[26] Even after those other obstacles had been interposed between East and West, there remained in many minds on both sides an undeniable if quite ambivalent sense of fraternity. Nothing more dramatically articulated its ambivalence in the East than the Byzantine attitude toward the Crusades.[27] Well before the Fourth Crusade, whenever Constantinople was in peril from the Arabs and then especially from the Turks, it had repeatedly appealed to the West for moral support and military intervention. But when the Western Catholic rescue had proved to be almost as great a terror as the Muslim threat had been, Byzantine statesmen and churchmen complained about the interference, as can be seen from the attitudes expressed by Princess Anna Comnena, writing her *Alexiad* in the first half of the twelfth century.[28]

By comparison with such complaints, the outcry over being violated in body and soul reached a new crescendo when brother Christians from the West captured the city and—in a violation of fraternal relations that can be seen as the real break—even established their own Latin monarchy and a Latin patriarchate in the person of the Venetian Tomaso Morosini.[29] But even a balanced account such as that of Donald E. Queller and Thomas F. Madden, just published in a revised edition by the University of Pennsylvania Press, makes the shocking facts unmistakable.[30] As Charles Dickens grimly paraphrased the motto of the French Revolution, "The Republic One and Indivisible of Liberty, Equality, Fraternity, or Death": "the last, much the easiest to bestow, O Guillotine!"[31] So, too, it proved to be in 1204 with the Church One and Indivisible! Although its horror is overshadowed by the Holocaust of the twentieth century, Sir Steven Runciman, who is in the unique position of being both an eminent historian of the Crusades and an authority on the schism between East and West, did feel able, even after World War II and the Holocaust, to express the judgment that "there was never a greater crime against humanity than the Fourth Crusade."[32]

Interestingly, Runciman's interpretation was affirmed in a recent "Editorial Notebook" of the *New York Times,* commenting on "The

Glory of Byzantium," an exhibit at the Metropolitan Museum of Art in New York:

> It is fair to say that Byzantium's most zealous tormentors lay in the Christian West, not the Islamic East. In 1204, the walls of Constantinople, which had withstood attacks by Persians, Arabs, Avars and Bulgars, fell to the Crusaders led by the craftiest of Venetian doges, Enrico Dondoldo, then about 85 and nearly blind, who led the way, shouting, through the breach. . . .
>
> Byzantium was fatally weakened by the invasion and the years of occupation that followed, opening the way for the Ottoman conquest in 1453 under Sultan Mehmet II.[33]

For the bearing of the Fourth Crusade on East-West estrangement, it is also necessary to ask, but it probably remains impossible to answer, a crucial question adapted and paraphrased from secular politics: What did the Pope know and when did he know it?[34] But it is clear that after the event Innocent III did reverse his earlier position and confirm the election of Morosini as Latin patriarch of Constantinople in 1205.[35]

800: Imperial Unity as "Ecumenical" Unity

If the Tradition that unites is in any decisive sense an imperial and hence a political tradition, so that "oikoumenē" means the Roman Empire—including the Christian Roman Empire governed from Constantinople as "New Rome" by an emperor who was "equal to the apostles"—then the ecumenical Tradition that unites moves from singular to plural, to traditions that divide and thus to a rupture, in the year 800, with the papal coronation of Charlemagne as Roman emperor.

Writing in 1928, S. Herbert Scott declared that although papal supremacy in 1054 and the Filioque in 867 were divisive if not decisive for the rupture,

> . . . the year 800 was the fateful year. The Christmas Day of that year, that saw the crown placed by the Pope upon the head of the

Emperor of the West, marked the turning-point. There were many roots of the Schism of Photius, afterwards consummated by Michael Caerularius, but the *chief cause* was the founding of the Frankish empire. It was intolerable to Byzantine pride. All the charges of heresy against the West are after-thoughts.[36]

This interpretation, considerably overstated though it is, makes the ecclesiastical relation between Latin Catholicism and Greek Orthodoxy a function of the political relation between West and East. The roots of this political situation lie in the fourth century, in the tension between the administrative division of the Roman Empire under Diocletian and the Christianization of the empire under Constantine. By moving the capital of the empire from Rome to Byzantium, Constantine was seeking not only to create a seat of government that was, in the words of a fifth-century Christian historian, "not polluted by altars, Grecian temples, or sacrifices,"[37] but to unify a vast realm whose integrity was threatened in its Eastern extremities by their isolation from the capital.[38] From the fourth to the sixth century, this notion of a single empire ruled by the *basileus* from Constantinople with an exarch in Ravenna as his surrogate had repeatedly proved itself subject to the same centrifugal forces which the emperor Diocletian had tried to overcome; Justinian strove, valiantly but quixotically, to enforce the notion of unity, and Boethius was probably a victim of that failure.[39]

Meanwhile, the demographic and military changes in the politics of the Western territories of the empire were redefining the situation also of the Church. At least in hindsight, it seems clear that when in 496 Clovis, king of the Franks, was converted to Catholic Christianity rather than to the Arian heresy professed by the Goths as a consequence of their having been converted by Ulfilas, the future of the West both politically and ecclesiastically would belong to a new alliance between the spiritual and the secular realms. Justinian's dream steadily became even less plausible than it already was, so that the imperial coronation of Charlemagne by Pope Leo III in the year 800 can be seen as the formal recognition of what was already a fait accompli in the realpolitik of the end of the eighth century.[40] But "ecumenical" and "imperial" had long been connected, at least since Constantine and Nicaea I.[41] As a result, there already was a fundamental divergence of opinion between East and West about what made a council ecumenical: for the East, an ecumenical council was convoked by the Christian emperor in Constantinople; for the West, an ecumenical council, howsoever it had been convoked, was ratified by the Pope.

Behind this explanation of the unity and the schism lies the tangled problem of the ecclesiological import of the political status of Constantinople as New Rome. Already at the First Council of Constantinople in 381, the standing of New Rome as a patriarchate of the Church was justified as a function of its standing as the new capital of the empire: "Because it is New Rome [*die to einai autēn nean Rōmēn*], the bishop of Constantinople is to enjoy the privileges of honour after the bishop of Rome"[42] That justification, however, achieved its most definitive and controversial formulation in the so-called twenty-eighth canon of the Council of Chalcedon in 451: "The fathers [at the Council of Constantinople in 381] rightly accorded prerogatives to the see of older Rome, *since that is an imperial city;* and moved by the same purpose the 150 most devout bishops apportioned equal prerogatives to the most holy see of new Rome, reasonably judging that *the city which is honoured by the imperial power and senate and enjoying privileges equalling older imperial Rome, should also be elevated to her level in ecclesiastical affairs and take second place after her.*"[43] Among the canon lawyers of the West, this twenty-eighth canon of Chalcedon was the subject of continuing debate, particularly but not exclusively in the controversies with the East, because it grounded the ecclesiastical status both of Old Rome and of New Rome in their political position as the capital cities of the empire.[44]

One additional factor, to which a posthumously published hypothesis of the great Belgian medievalist, Henri Pirenne, called attention exactly sixty years ago, was the historical connection between Muhammad and Charlemagne as an explanation of the schism.[45] During the century between the death of the prophet in 632 and Charles Martel's checking of the Muslim advance at the Battle of Tours and Poitiers in 732, Islam had spread south and west from the Arabian Peninsula across all of historically Christian North Africa, whether Greek or Coptic or Latin, and on into Spain and Gaul. Three of the five patriarchates that defined the Eastern theory of pentarchy came under Muslim rule—Jerusalem and Antioch in 638, Alexandria in

641—leaving only Constantinople and Rome as the two surviving patriarchal sees whose civil government was in Christian hands. Among all the other political, economic, and military implications of this Muslim expansion was the even further isolation of the patriarchates of Rome and New Rome from each other. And ecclesiastically, the bishop of Rome and *pontifex maximus,* as the real heir of the Caesars in the West even without the forged Donation of Constantine to back his claims, was likewise acknowledging a fait accompli in the realpolitik of both state and church when he crowned Charlemagne as emperor at the old Basilica of Saint Peter in the year 800.

1576: Ritual Diversity under Apostolic Unity with Rome

If diverse rituals are regarded as not necessarily traditions that divide, so long as they are kept within the context of the unifying Tradition represented by apostolic unity in communion with the see of Rome, then the chain of events between Florence in 1439 and Brest in 1596 marks the definitive break.

The problem of ritual diversity under apostolic unity with Rome had been playing a major part in the exacerbation of relations between Eastern and Western Christendom, especially since the disputes evoked by the Moravian mission in the ninth century, which had coincided both with the eruption of the Filioque and with the Photian schism.[46] The Slavonic liturgy was the gift of the apostles to the Slavs, Saints Constantine-Cyril and Methodius, who had probably grown up bilingual in Thessalonica, perhaps because they had a Slavic mother, and who came to Moravia from Constantinople. It was not the policy of Constantinople to impose the Greek text of the *Liturgy of Saint John Chrysostom* or the *Liturgy of Saint Basil* on its converts, but, in what the distinguished scholar of Slavic linguistics Alexander M. Schenker has recently described as "the most momentous event in the history of the Slavs," to translate them into the newly codified language we now call Old Church Slavonic.[47] In the eyes of some in the West, that philosophy of missions and of liturgy was interpreted as fostering traditions that divided, colliding head-on with the practice of enforcing the Latin Mass, which was interpreted as the Tradition that united—united the

Western Church, that is. Western opponents of the Slavonic liturgy espoused the theory of trilingualism, that the only three languages in which the Divine Liturgy could legitimately be celebrated were the languages on the cross, which according to the Gospel (John 19:20) were Hebrew (i.e., Aramaic), Latin, and Greek; Cyril and Methodius took the case to Rome. When the dust had finally settled, the Slavic-speaking peoples had been divided between those (notably Russia, Ukraine, Serbia, and Bulgaria) who followed Cyril and Methodius in keeping the Slavonic liturgy but at the price of union with the see of Rome, and those (notably Poland, Bohemia, Croatia, and Slovakia), who followed Cyril and Methodius in accepting the authority of Rome but at the price of the Slavonic liturgy.

An interesting symbol of this issue is the equivocal translation of the Greek word *doxa:* to mean "belief, opinion," as it does in a celebrated passage of Plato's *Timaeus* where, as "mere belief," it is contrasted with *nous*, "reason," and *alētheia*, "truth";[48] or to mean "glory," as in the Greek of the *Gloria Patri*. Now depending on which meaning of *doxa* one took, *orthodoxia* could mean "right belief" or "right worship" (or, of course, both). The Sunday of Orthodoxy on the first Sunday of Great Lent in the Eastern calendar commemorates not the orthodoxy of the dogma of Nicaea in 325 nor the orthodoxy of the dogma of Chalcedon in 451, but the orthodoxy of the restoration of the icons in 843. The translation of *doxa* in liturgical Church Slavonic and its later Slavic cognates as *slava* ("glory") made Orthodoxy, *Pravoslavie,* as the Tradition that unites, the Eastern equivalent of *lex orandi* as well as *lex credendi*. From this it followed that to be Orthodox meant to teach aright and to give glory aright; but each of the autocephalous Orthodox churches developed some of its own particular traditions for meeting this requirement—particular traditions that in the Eastern context did not, however, become traditions that divide.

Seen in that framework, the relation between the liturgical, dogmatic, and jurisdictional decrees of the Council of Florence provides a striking case study of the problem of this lecture.[49] The union principles of *Laetentur caeli* of July 1439 affirmed that diverse rituals were not necessarily traditions that divide, so long as they were kept within the context of the unifying Tradition of communion with the see of Rome; the Filioque, too, was finessed by equating it with "ex Patre per

Filium."[50] But the judgments of Orthodox historians on the Union of Florence are uniformly negative.[51] It is seen as the result of a compromise, brought about within the West by the pressure of the Great Schism between Rome and Avignon and by the conflict between papacy and council, and brought about within the East by the pressure of the Ottoman Turks as well as by the lingering aftereffects of the Latin sack of Constantinople in 1204.[52] In Byzantium, as Deno Geneakoplos has summarized it, "the popular opposition was based . . . on the belief that union had been obtained under duress, that the military aid agreed to by the Holy See would, like previous papal promises, be ineffectual, and, finally, on the conviction that the Byzantine people themselves would suffer the judgment of God if the purity of the faith were altered."[53] The Muscovite objections to the Union, by which its implementation was effectively blocked and which were followed closely by the establishment of the patriarchate of Moscow in 1589, constituted in some respects the most decisive veto of Florence.[54] If (a big "if"!) Florence was a genuine union or reunion, then it can be argued that the dates of its rejection are the actual dates of the schism.[55]

But as the Union of Florence came to grief in the territories of *Rus'*, so it was also in the territories of *Rus'* that it achieved, more than a century later, a permanent if highly controversial ratification, in the Union of Brest of 1596.[56] Ruthenia/Ukraine, in the Union of 1596, was seeking a way to break out of the dilemma of the Slavs which I described earlier—keeping the Slavonic liturgy but at the price of union with the see of Rome, or affirming the supremacy of Rome but at the price of the Slavonic liturgy—by having it both ways.[57] As its twentieth-century Metropolitan, Andrej Šeptyckyj declared to the Austrian Parliament on 28 June 1910 that the Ukrainian Catholic Church was (as it is again today, after the fall of the Soviet Union and the nullification of the so-called Synod of L'viv of 8–10 March 1946) "the largest group anywhere of adherents to the Union of Florence, who 'preserve the worthiest ancient traditions of early Christianity, namely, the principle of the union of the Western and Eastern Churches.'"[58] Other Ukrainian Catholic spokesmen such as Cardinal Josyf Slipyj made a point of reminding both the Roman Catholics and the Orthodox that it was a patriarch of Constantinople, Cyril Lukar, who had, in the name of the Tradition that unites, issued a confession of faith that innovated and divided by its concessions to Calvinist doctrine,[59] but that it was a metropolitan of Kiev, Petro Mohyla (who has now been canonized as a saint), who vindicated the Orthodox and Catholic faith as the Tradition that unites, in *The Orthodox Confession of the Catholic and Apostolic Eastern Church* of 1638, published in 1645.[60] It was an effort to rehabilitate the union principles of the Council of Florence by condemning separatism on one side and Latinization on the other, and thus to articulate the very distinction with which we have been working here between the Tradition that unites and the traditions that divide, when on 30 November 1894 Pope Leo XIII issued *Orientalium dignitas ecclesiarum.*[61]

1341–1368: Unity of the Spirit Despite Fundamental Differences of Spirituality

If fundamental (and contradictory?) differences of spirituality cannot coexist under the protective aegis of "the unity of the Spirit in the bond of peace" (Eph. 4:3), which is the Tradition that unites, and if thereby such differences become traditions that divide, then the Eastern adoption and the Western condemnation of Palamite-Hesychast spirituality in 1341–1368 raised (another) wall of separation between East and West.

No historian would seriously propose 1341–1368 as *the* date of the separation. But if, as many historians would seriously contend, spirituality can be more important than either polity or dogma in defining the Tradition that unites as well as the traditions that divide, then, in addition to the other barriers we have been itemizing, the formal approval of Palamite doctrine by Constantinople in 1341 and his canonization in 1368, with the Western condemnation of that doctrine, provides interesting and important insights into the relation between the unity of the Spirit as the Tradition that unites and differences of spirituality as traditions that divide. In his massive compilation of the dogmatic differences between the Eastern and the Western churches, therefore, Martin Jugie has brought together the official actions of the so-called Palamite councils of 1341, as well as the Western responses, and has identified the Palamite doctrine of the divine *energeia*, as distinct from either the one divine *ousia* or the three divine *hypostaseis*, as an additional Eastern tradition that divides and therefore as a barrier between the two communities.[62]

It is central to the spirituality of Saint Gregory Palamas and the distinctive teaching of the Eastern councils supporting him that beyond this question of the divine energies and their metaphysical-ontological status in trinitarian doctrine,[63] a basic difference between the two spiritualities can be seen in their diverging ways of dealing with the transfiguration of Christ (*metamorphōsis* in Greek, *preobraženie* in Russian), because the specific divine *energeia* under discussion was the "uncreated light" that shone on Mount Tabor at the transfiguration.[64] Western interpreters of this event in the life of Christ have often focused their attention on its place within the dramaturgy of the Gospels, as a prelude to the passion narrative: just as the baptism of Jesus at the very beginning of His ministry was an attestation of His mission, as defined by the voice from heaven "This is my Son, the Beloved" (Matt. 3:17), so again His transfiguration was a vindication of His divine credentials, with the voice from heaven repeating the words "This is my Son, the Beloved" (Matt. 17:5). Those same accents appear in Eastern expositions as well, but instead of being one in a series of miracles, the transfiguration becomes a key both to Christology and to salvation-as-*theōsis*.[65] A representative example is the exposition of the transfiguration attributed to Saint John of Damascus.[66]

Because the transfigured human nature of Christ was, for this spirituality, a revelation of perfect human nature when it is deified—as the New Testament could be taken to be saying, by a conflation of 2 Peter 1:4 and 1 John 3:2—the meaning of the saving work of Christ was not comprehended by the Western preoccupation with the *satisfactio* rendered to the violated honor or *rectitudo* of God by the death of One who, being both God and man, could pay a satisfaction that availed for all—a theory that was systematized by Saint Anselm of Canterbury and that survived, and was even reinforced by, the Lutheran and Calvinist Reformations. Already in the fourth century, Saint Gregory of Nazianzus had criticized such a definition of the work of Christ as *ekdikēsis* on the grounds that "there is something humiliating in the very idea."[67] As expressed liturgically, this difference of spirituality between East and West has continued long after Nazianzen and Anselm, and after Palamas and Barlaam. Was it a recognition of the centrality of this difference of spirituality between East and West, as a tradition that divides, when the Palamite synods of 1341–1368 made Hesychasm official and when the West made it heretical? Or is it significant that, in Father Florovsky's formulation, "the question about the *ultimate motive* of the Incarnation was never formally discussed in the Patristic Age,"[68] with the result that the Tradition that unites, in the very same ecumenical councils still affirmed by both East and West, did not focus primary attention on the *work* of Christ but on the *person* of Christ, defining in great detail that He was "begotten, not made" as Nicaea confessed in 325 and that the two natures in Him were united with "no confusion, no change, no division, no separation" as Chalcedon declared in 451, but not defining with any similar specificity how it was that all of this had happened "for our salvation" as Nicaea said? And can that difference within the texts of the creeds mean that the dogma of the person of Christ is the Tradition that unites, but that doctrines of the work of Christ, including even the concepts of salvation as either *satisfactio* or *theōsis*, should not become traditions that divide?

Now I do not, of course, imagine that fixing a precise date for the schism between the East and the West is a very important question in itself, nor one whose resolution would as such bring the churches any closer together. Indeed, I do not believe that any scholarly study, whether of tradition or of liturgy or even of Scripture, can by itself overcome these divisions, which have so many complex causes and which have taken so many centuries to develop. But I am convinced that the shortest distance between two positions is often the study of the past, and therefore that without such study we are doomed to perpetuating the divisions, or to sentimentalizing them (which is not much better), unless we study our several pasts together. It is my hope and earnest prayer that the monument here at Tantur to the historic meeting in 1964 between Patriarch Athenagoras I and Pope Paul VI may, in the providence of God, continue to make its blessed contribution to this end:

Veni, Creator Spiritus!

Notes

1. Thomas Stransky, "Tantur Ecumenical Institute," *Dictionary of the Ecumenical Movement* (Geneva and Grand Rapids, 1991), 970.

2. I am elaborating here on material that I presented orally to the Orthodox-Catholic Theological Discussion at its fiftieth meeting, on 26 October 1995, in Milwaukee, Wisconsin, at the invitation of His Excellency, Archbishop Rembert Weakland, O.S.B.

3. Georges V. Florovsky, "Patriarch Jeremiah II and the Lutheran Divines" and "The Greek Version of the Augsburg Confession," *Collected Works* (Belmont, Mass., 1972–), 2:143–60, 240–41 (notes).

4. Edward Gibbon, *The History of the Decline and Fall of the Roman Empire*, ch. 60, ed. J. B. Bury, 7 vols. (London, 1896–1900), 6:370.

5. Jōannēs Karmirēs, *Ta dogmatika kai symbolika mnēmeia tēs orthodoxou katholikēs ekklēsias*, 2 vols. (Athens, 1952–53), 1:285–94. (Hereafter abbreviated as "Karmirēs").

6. "Michael abusivus patriarcha neophytus [cum suis] . . . sint anathema . . . et cum omnibus haereticis, imo cum diabolo et angelis eius, nisi forte respuerint. Amen, Amen, Amen." See the account in Martin Jugie, *Le schism byzantin: aperçu historique et doctrinal* (Paris, 1941), 203–8: "La sentence d'excommunication contre Michel Cérulaire et ses partisans (16 juillet 1054)."

7. Cf. Anton Michel, *Humbert und Kerullarios* (Paderborn, 1924–30), with substantial documentation.

8. One of the few modern studies of Michael Cerularius is Mahlon H. Smith, *And Taking Bread . . . : Cerularius and the Azyme Controversy of 1054* (Paris, 1978).

9. See the thoughtful comments of Venance Grumel, *The Schism of Michael Cerularius in 1054* (Garrison, N.Y., 1954).

10. F. E. Brightman, *Liturgies Eastern and Western* (Oxford, 1896), 317; 574–75.

11. Maurice Gordillo, "Photius et primatus Romanus," *Orientalis Christiana Periodica* 6 (1940): 1–39.

12. Francis Dvornik, *The Idea of Apostolicity in Byzantium and the Legend of the Apostle Andrew* (Cambridge, Mass., 1958); John Meyendorff, "St. Peter in Byzantine Theology," *The Primacy of Peter* (London, 1963), 7–29.

13. A magisterial discussion is that of Walter Ullmann, *The Growth of Papal Government in the Middle Ages: A Study in the Ideological Relation of Clerical to Lay Power*, 2d ed. (London, 1962).

14. Karmirēs, 2:896–97.

15. Both (or several) sides are presented in Lukas Vischer, ed., *Spirit of God, Spirit of Christ: Ecumenical Reflections on the Filioque Controversy* (Geneva, 1981); for a rather optimistic view of recent research, see Maria-Helena Gamillscheg, *Die Kontroverse um das Filioque: Möglichkeiten einer Problemlösung*

auf Grund der Forschungen und Gespräche der letzten hundert Jahre (Würzburg, 1996).

16. George C. Berthold, "Maximus Confessor and the *Filioque*," *Studia Patristica*, 18:1 (1985), 113–17.

17. See the learned and polemical discussion and the copious bibliography in *Dictionnaire de théologie Catholique* (Paris, 1903–50), 5:2309–45.

18. Gregory the Great *Epistolae* II.26.2 (*PL* 76:1198).

19. Peter Brown, *Augustine of Hippo: A Biography* (London, 1967), 36, 273. The question is considered pro and con in the context of the problems of tradition, transmission, and translation by Berthold Altaner's *Kleine patristische Schriften* (Berlin, 1967).

20. Augustine *De Trinitate* V.viii.10 (*CCSL* 50:216–17); also VII.vi.11 (*CCSL* 50:261–62).

21. See Hans-Jürgen Marx, *Filioque und Verbot eines anderen Glaubens auf dem Florentinum: Zum Pluralismus in dogmatischen Formeln* (Sankt Augustin, 1977).

22. Owen Chadwick, *From Bossuet to Newman: The Idea of Doctrinal Development* (Cambridge, 1957), 235; italics added.

23. Francis Dvornik, *The Photian Schism: History and Legend* (Cambridge, Mass., 1948), 120–23.

24. There is a convenient summary in J. N. D. Kelly, *Early Christian Creeds* (London, 1952), 196–331.

25. Aristeides Papadakis, *Crisis in Byzantium: The Filioque Controversy in the Patriarchate of Gregory II of Cyprus* (New York, 1983).

26. For a vivid account, see Alfred J. Andrea, "The *Devastatio Constantinopolitana,* A Special Perspective on the Fourth Crusade: An Analysis, New Edition, and Translation," *Historical Reflections* 19 (1993): 107–49.

27. Basile G. Spiridonakis, *Grecs, Occidentaux et Turcs de 1054 à 1453: quatre siècles d'histoire de relations internationales* (Thessaloniki, 1990).

28. Anna Comnena, *Alexiad,* XIV.ii, tr. E.R.A. Sewter (Harmondsworth, 1969), 438–39.

29. L. Santifaller, *Beiträge zur Geschichte des lateinischen Patriarchats von Konstantinopel (1204–1261)* (Weimar, 1938).

30. Donald E. Queller and Thomas F. Madden, *The Fourth Crusade: The Conquest of Constantinople,* rev. ed. (Philadelphia, 1997).

31. Charles Dickens, *A Tale of Two Cities,* bk. III, ch. 4, ed. George Woodcock (Harmondsworth, 1970), 301, 304.

32. Steven Runciman, *A History of the Crusades,* 3 vols. (Cambridge, 1951–54), 3:131. See also John Godfrey, *1204, The Unholy Crusade* (Oxford, 1980).

33. Karl E. Meyer, "The West's Debt to Byzantium," *New York Times* (30 March 1997), News of the Week in Review, 10.

34. The question is set into the context of the Pope's relation to the Crusades by Helmut Roscher, *Papst Innocenz III. und die Kreuzzüge* (Göttingen,

1969); and into the larger context of Innocent's pontificate by James M. Powell, ed., *Innocent III: Vicar of Christ or Lord of the World?* 2d ed. (Washington, 1994).

35. Alfred John Andrea, "Pope Innocent III as Crusader and Canonist: His Relations with the Greeks of Constantinople" (Ph.D. diss., Cornell University, 1969); B. A. Pančenko, *Latinskij Konstantinopol i papa Innokentij III* (Odessa, 1914), 12–44; Achille Luchaire, *Innocent III: La question d'Orient* (Paris, 1907).

36. S. Herbert Scott, *The Eastern Churches and the Papacy* (London, 1928), 310; italics original.

37. Sozomen *Historia ecclesiastica* II.3 (GCS 50:51-54).

38. There is an incisive summary in John Meyendorff, *Imperial Unity and Christian Divisions: The Church 450–680 A.D.* (Crestwood, N.Y., 1989), 5–38.

39. Boethius *De consolatione philosophiae* IP4.20–21 (*CCSL* 94:9); see Henry Chadwick, *Boethius: The Consolations of Music, Logic, Theology, and Philosophy* (Oxford, 1981), 55.

40. Peter Classen, *Karl der Grosse, das Papsttum und Byzanz: Die Begründung des karolingischen Kaisertums* (Sigmaringen, 1985).

41. Passages collected in G. W. H. Lampe, ed., *A Patristic Greek Lexicon* (Oxford, 1961), 944–45.

42. Council of Constantinople (381), canon 3, *Decrees of the Ecumenical Councils,* ed. Norman P. Tanner, 2 vols. (Washington, 1990), 1:32.

43. Council of Chalcedon (451), canon 28 in Tanner, *Ecumenical Councils,* 1:100; italics added.

44. Thomas Owen Martin, "The Twenty-Eighth Canon of Chalcedon: A Background Note," in Aloys Grillmeier and Heinrich Bacht, eds., *Das Konzil von Chalkedon: Geschichte und Gegenwart,* 3 vols. (Würzburg, 1951), 2:433–58.

45. Henri Pirenne, *Mahomet et Charlemagne* (Paris, 1937). For discussions of it, which are unfortunately largely confined to economics, see Alfred F. Havighurst, ed., *The Pirenne Thesis: Analysis, Criticism, and Revision* (Boston, 1958).

46. Francis Dvornik, *Byzantine Missions among the Slavs: SS. Constantine-Cyril and Methodius* (New Brunswick, N.J., 1970).

47. Alexander M. Schenker, *The Dawn of Slavic: An Introduction to Slavic Philology* (New Haven, 1995), 26.

48. Plato *Timaeus* 51 D-E.

49. Building on the pioneering studies of Joseph Gill, a distinguished group of scholars have collaborated on *Firenze e il Concilio del 1439,* ed. Paolo Viti (Florence, 1994).

50. Denzinger 1300–1308; Giuseppe Alberigo, ed., *Christian Unity: The Council of Ferrara-Florence 1438/39* (Louvain, 1991).

51. The Eastern interest in reunion is described in the brief study of Damaskinos Papandreou, *Die Konzilien von Basel und Ferrara-Florenz* (Basel, 1992).

52. Ivan N. Ostroumoff, *The History of the Council of Florence,* tr. Basil Popoff (Boston, 1971).

53. Deno John Geneakoplos, "The Council of Florence (1438–39) and the Problem of Union between the Byzantine and Latin Churches," *Byzantine East and Latin West: Two Worlds of Christendom in Middle Ages and Renaissance* (New York, 1966), 84–109.

54. These objections and their history are conveniently summarized in the lengthy supplementary entry, "Florentinskaja unija; pop'itki sojedinenija s' Zapadnoj Cerkovju na Vostoku i v Rossij. Uniat'i," *Polnyj pravoslavnyj bogoslavskij enciklopedičeskij slovar',* 2 vols., [1913] reprint ed. (London, 1971), 2:2446–54. Documents and analysis in Joannes Krajčar, ed. *Acta Slavica Concilii Florentini* (Rome, 1976).

55. See also Josef Macha, *Ecclesiastical Unification: A Theoretical Framework together with Case Studies from the History of Latin-Byzantine Relations* (Rome, 1974), which relates it to the Union of Brest.

56. Still useful is Oscar Halecki, *From Florence to Brest (1439–1596)* (New York, 1958).

57. Ihor Mončak, *Florentine ecumenism in the Kyivan Church* (Rome, 1987).

58. Gregor Prokoptschuk, *Metropolit Graf Scheptyćky,* 2d ed. (Munich, 1967), 133–37.

59. Cyril Lucar, *Confessio fidei reverendissimi domini Cyrilli Patriarchae Constantinopolitani nomine et consensu Patriarcharum Alexandrii et Hierosolymitani, aliarumque Ecclesiarum orientalium Antistitum* (Karmirēs 2:565–70). There is an English translation in Charles King Bradow, "The Career and Confession of Cyril Loukaris: The Greek Orthodox Church and Its Relations with Western Christians (1543–1638)" (Ph.D. diss., Ohio State University, 1960), 190–204.

60. Karmirēs 2:593-686. Petro Mohyla, *The Orthodox Confession of the Catholic and Apostolic Eastern Church* (London, 1898).

61. *ASS* 27:257–64; Rosario F. Esposito, *Leone XIII et l'Oriente cristiano: studi storico–sistematico* (Rome, 1961).

62. Martin Jugie, *Theologia dogmatica Christianorum Orientalium ab ecclesia Catholica dissidentium,* 5 vols. (Paris, 1926–35), 1:436–42; 2:48–183.

63. Michael Andrew Fahey and John Meyendorff, *Trinitarian Theology East and West: St. Thomas Aquinas–St. Gregory Palamas* (Brookline, Mass., 1977).

64. Georges Habra, *La transfiguration selon les pères grecs* (Paris, 1974).

65. Gēorgios I. Mantzardēs, *The Deification of Man: St. Gregory Palamas and the Orthodox Tradition,* tr. Liadain Sherrard, foreword by Bishop Kallistos of Diokleia (Crestwood, N.Y., 1984).

66. "Homilia in Transfigurationem Domini" (PG 96:545–76).

67. Gregory of Nazianzus *Orationes* xxx.14 (SC 250:256).

68. Florovsky, *Collected Works* (Belmont, Mass., 1972) 3:164; italics original.

The Traditions That Divide, the Tradition That Unites   23

TWO

The Churches in the Middle East

Frans Bouwen

∞

For Christians coming to the Middle East to meet the churches of this region is somehow like coming home. It means going back to the very roots of their faith and church life. Indeed, it is here that everything started: the whole story of the Bible, the ministry, death and resurrection of Christ, the beginnings of the early Church as they are known through the Acts of the Apostles, and also the formation of the first great Christian traditions.

However, coming home to the churches in the Middle East is never going back to a past that lies very far behind us. In fact, in the Middle East, traditions are very much alive today. Here history never belongs to the past and one does not have to look backwards to find it. For instance, the Council of Chalcedon (451) is almost forgotten in the West. Who remembers it and who cares about it, except a few experts? By contrast, in the churches of the Middle East, Chalcedon is very much present. It is as if it happened yesterday, or even this morning, because the reception or the refusal of Chalcedon is part and parcel of the identity of these churches and a concrete expression of their faithfulness to Christ.

This may sound surprising to many Westerners coming to the Middle East. Often their first impression is that traditions are valued for themselves here, are no more than relics of a distant past, no longer able to communicate life today. This shock will be even greater for Evangelical, reborn Christians, to whom a person, a community or a tradition that does not rest on such a very personal experience does not appear to be Christian. It is therefore of fundamental importance for Western visitors—especially on their first visit—to try to go beyond these first impressions, in order to discover how personal faith and community life are entirely integrated in the East and how tradition is like a living community that includes not only the whole life of the faithful living today but also the many generations who form an unbroken chain going back to the Apostles.

The diversity of the many traditions coexisting side by side in the Middle East is one of the main factors contributing to this first impression of confusion. Why so many different traditions, for such small communities living together in such a limited space? Is it not an additional proof that these traditions have in fact lost their *raison d'être,* have lost contact with reality? Some theologians may even be inclined to jump to the conclusion that such a multiplicity of traditions and jurisdictions is nonsensical, from the ecclesiological point of view, being against the fundamental principle of one bishop in one place.

In order to rediscover the true meaning of this diversity, it is important to realize that each of these church traditions is a particular inculturation of the Gospel in a particular country, nation, language, culture, long before the term "inculturation" existed. From the very beginning, the Gospel met many very ancient and rich cultures in this region: Greek, Syriac, Armenian, Egyptian, etc. In each of these cultures, the Gospel was proclaimed, the mysteries of God's love were celebrated in the liturgy, and theological reflection was initiated. It is important to become aware of this very ancient reality at a time when in theological and ecumenical circles there is so much talk going on about "Gospel and cultures." In the Middle East that reality existed long before the existence of the present-day terminology.

Therefore each of the present traditions has its homeland, where it was born and developed: Mesopotamia, Armenia, the great province of Syria, Byzantium, Egypt. Only later, as a consequence of the difficult historical circumstances—wars, persecutions—these peoples started migrating in search of survival. The churches and traditions moved along with their peoples and so, little by little, ended up by living to-gether in the same places. In these new surroundings, the great diversity is less easy to understand and to justify, but we should realize that exactly these traditions played an essential role in keeping these communities together and preserving their faithfulness to the Gospel in changing situations.

Unfortunately, these diversities at times also became divisions, par-ticularly after the councils of Ephesus (431) and Chalcedon (451). The divisions in the aftermath of Chalcedon had tragic consequences for the Christian presence in the Middle East. Six centuries later came the great division between East and West. Anyhow, as Westerners we have to acknowledge that we also contributed to the diversities and the divisions of the Christians in this region. From the sixteenth century onwards, different attempts were made to re-establish unity between the Church of Rome and the churches in the East, but most of them failed and, in fact, resulted in new divisions. This helps to explain the difficult position of the Oriental Catholic churches today in the new ecumenical context. Other missionary efforts, especially from the last century on, led to the creation of other new communities, mainly Anglican and Protestant, built up not with non-Christians who con-verted but with baptized persons coming from the ancient traditional churches.

Panorama of the Existing Churches

When it comes to presenting a brief survey of the different churches that are present in the Middle East today, the most convenient way seems to be the framework adopted by the Middle East Council of Churches (MECC), built on the idea of four families of churches.

1. The Oriental Orthodox family: comprising the non-Chalcedonian Churches, formerly called the "Monophysite" Churches
2. The Eastern Orthodox family: comprising the Chalcedonian or Byzan-tine or Greek Orthodox Churches
3. The Catholic family

4. The Evangelical and Episcopal family
- Outside this original framework (and outside the MECC until 1995) there is still the Assyrian Church of the East, formerly called the "Nestorian" Church.

Let us now have a quick look at the main churches belonging to these four families.

The Oriental Orthodox Family

In the Oriental Orthodox family, the first church is the *Coptic Church* of Egypt, with its center in Alexandria and Cairo. Very proud of the greatness of its history, with the famous theological School of Alexandria and the important role played in the origins of monasticism, the Coptic Church also has a very long history of living together with Islam. It is by far the biggest church in the Middle East, having in fact a greater number of faithful than all the other churches put together.

Then comes the *Syrian Orthodox Church,* which has its center at present in Damascus, Syria. This church is proud that it uses in its liturgy the language spoken by Christ; up to the present day, a variation of the language is still spoken in numerous Syriac communities. In this church monasticism occupies an important place, to the point of being the center of the life of the church and the guardian of its cultural and spiritual tradition. In the past this church played a central role in the translation into Arabic and the transmission of the Greek and Byzantine literature and civilization shortly after the Islamic conquests. At present this community suffers from a very strong emigration from the region, mainly due to the fact that it lives in contested places, for instance in the center of the conflict between Turkey and Kurdish nationalists. There is a real danger that the historical homeland of this church, in the Southeast of Turkey, may not have any Christians left in the near future.

The *Armenian Orthodox Church* rightly points out that Armenia was the first nation in history to adopt Christianity (in 301). The Armenian Church is preparing to celebrate the seventeenth centenary in 2001. Living at the crossroads between Byzantium, Syria, and Persia, Armenia was very often caught up in the conflicts between its neighbors, with the Armenian genocide in the beginning of this century being the climax. Suffering and martyrdom became part and parcel of Armenian spirituality. In the Middle East, there are two distinct Armenian Orthodox jurisdictions: the Catholicate of the House of Cilicia, with its center in Lebanon, and the Patriarchate of Jerusalem.

The Eastern Orthodox Family

The Eastern Orthodox family comprises in the first place the *Patriarchate of Alexandria*, which has had a very rich history and tradition. However at present, there is only a little flock of faithful left in Egypt (Greek and Arabic speaking). A recent new development is the fact that, in different places and under very different circumstances, African Orthodox communities were formed in several parts of Africa. Perhaps these African Orthodox are already now more numerous than the Greeks. The late Patriarch Parthenios III, who died in 1996, was not afraid to say that the Greek Orthodox Patriarchate of Alexandria is on its way to becoming a predominantly African Patriarchate, and that it is a gift of God's providence.

The second church of the Eastern Orthodox Family is the *Patriarchate of Antioch*, which in history played a central role as link between the Greek or Byzantine, the Syriac, and the Mesopotamian traditions. Now it plays a similar role as link with the Arab and Islamic world and culture. About fifty years ago, the Orthodox Youth Movement started a radical renewal that little by little has touched the whole church community. The Greek Orthodox Patriarchate of Antioch, leaders and lay people, were able to play an inspiring role in the ecumenical field, both in the MECC and in the relations between the churches on the local level in Lebanon and Syria.

The third church of the Eastern Orthodox family, the *Patriarchate of Jerusalem,* plays a humble and unique role, because of the historical and symbolic significance of Jerusalem, and is living on the threshold of many new developments in the region.

The *Church of Cyprus*, although usually not included in the Middle East as such, is the fourth church of the Eastern Orthodox family. It has its own ancient history and its own specific problems today.

The Catholic Family

The Catholic family regroups six Oriental Catholic churches and one Latin church.

The *Maronite Church* is the only Oriental tradition of the Middle East that is entirely in communion with the Church of Rome. Being of the West-Syrian tradition, Maronites are inseparably linked with Lebanon, so much so that one could say that the Maronites have made Lebanon, and Lebanon has made the Maronites.

The other Oriental Catholic churches in the region—the *Greek Catholic, Syrian Catholic, Coptic Catholic, Armenian Catholic,* and *Chaldean*—endeavour to remain faithful to the liturgical and spiritual traditions of the Orthodox church with which they have a common origin. Each of these Catholic churches has its own history, but nevertheless it may be said that they have this in common, that they are the outcome of an attempt to re-establish unity between West and East, an attempt that failed and so led to a new division. However, their relations with the corresponding Orthodox churches are very different from what is going on at present in Central and Eastern Europe; on the whole these relations are becoming more frequent and sometimes result in a real pastoral collaboration on grass-roots levels.

The *Latin Church* is present almost everywhere in the Middle East, but it is only in Jerusalem and the Holy Land that a real Arab-speaking Latin community developed. It is the result of a long and active presence of expatriate Latin priests, religious, and sisters in the region, especially around the Holy Places. Lately the Latin Church has become an active participant in the local and regional ecumenical activities.

In this framework can also be mentioned the *Assyrian Church of the East,* formerly also called the "Nestorian Church." Why here? The reason is simple. The Common Christological Declaration, signed by Pope John Paul II and Patriarch Denkha IV in November 1994, opened new ways for relationships and collaboration and, as a result, the Assyrian Church could become a member of the MECC as a part of the Catholic family. Following its own, East-Syrian tradition, outside the Byzantine Empire, and rich in martyrs, the Assyrian Church has known an extraordinary missionary expansion as far as China, between the seventh and thirteenth centuries. As a consequence of dramatic historic circumstances, especially in the first half of this century, this church has seen its members reduced to a small number, the large majority of them living in a worldwide diaspora.

The Evangelical and Episcopal Family

The Evangelical and Episcopal churches are the fourth church family. They are characterized by a great diversity related to their various cultural backgrounds, theological traditions, and historical relations to missionary agencies. The largest Protestant group comprises the Evangelical reformed churches which grew up among the Armenians, Copts and Syrians, then follow the Anglican or Episcopal and Lutheran traditions.

Middle East Council of Churches

The present structure of the MECC is the outcome of seventy years of history, marked by two lines of development. A first line goes from expatriate to a local Middle Eastern involvement. The second line goes gradually from missionary agencies to churches. The main dates of these developments:

1925: Creation in Jerusalem of the "Near East Christian Council for Missionary Cooperation," regrouping Protestant missionary agencies in view of cooperation

1932: Creation of the "Near East Christian Council," integrating into the former organization the newly constituted Evangelical communities of the Middle East

1962: The missionary agencies withdraw and the local Episcopal and Evangelical churches constitute the "Near East Council of Churches," with the Syrian Orthodox Church as the only Oriental church taking part

1974: Creation of the present "Middle East Council of Churches" based on the principle of three families of churches: Oriental Orthodox churches, Eastern Orthodox churches and Evangelical and Episcopal churches.

1989: By becoming full members, the Catholic churches constitute the
fourth family of churches.

It seems important to explain briefly this concept of "families of
churches," three at the beginning of the MECC, four at present with
the Catholics. What is the reason and meaning?

In fact, the principle tries to find a subtle balance in representation in the governing bodies of the council between, on the one hand,
the number of churches, which would be in favor of the Protestant
churches, and, on the other hand, the number of faithful largely in
favor of the Orthodox churches. Each family has the same number of
representatives both in the General Assembly and in the Executive
Committee. Thanks to this principle, no single church or family of
churches can exercise a predominant influence in the council. This
has certainly helped in promoting mutual trust and collaboration.

This structure of church families offers, in my opinion, something
quite unique, and, above all, it seems to work! Would it not be worthwhile to reflect upon it, in view of possible applications elsewhere? For
instance, could it not be a way of getting around some of the problems
for a full participation of the Roman Catholic Church in the World
Council of Churches? Now the WCC is built on the representation of
the local churches, while independent local churches do not exist in
the WCC. Could the church families be an answer to it? Of course,
other problems would come up. However, would it not be worthwhile
to consider this example in the framework of the ongoing reflection on
"common understanding and vision" of the WCC?

How representative is the MECC? At present, the very large majority of the churches and confessions with local membership are
represented in the MECC. This is very important for its significance,
its activities, and its contacts with civil authorities or representatives
of other religions. Baptists, Pentecostals, and Evangelicals are not yet
members. However, I think it may be said that the MECC has tried to
establish contacts with most of these communities or movements,
with limited response or success.

Another very important characteristic of the MECC seems to be the
high level of involvement of the churches. For instance, at the General
Assembly most of the heads of churches are present: Patriarchs, bish-

ops, presidents of synods, etc. Such a presence is very impressive and offers the image of a real gathering of churches. The presidents of the council, who are ex officio members of the Executive Committee, are also heads of churches, and they are actively involved in the decisions and initiatives. Of course, this does not mean that everything is perfect; some initiatives still may seem remote from the churches' life, but a serious reflection is going on, in connection with the need for reorganization and funding problems.

Most of the main orientations of the MECC are to a large extent identical with the main concerns of the churches. Mentioning them here can spare me the necessity of repeating it for the single churches.

(1) There is, in the first place, a constant concern for the respect of the richness of the diversity of the many traditions. As I already pointed out, these traditions are part and parcel of the identity of the churches, and unity or collaboration can never require abandoning one's identity. These traditions have also been a major factor in the survival of the churches during past centuries amidst very difficult circumstances, and they will undoubtedly still play an important role in working for the future of the Christian presence in the Middle East. Of course, this supposes that these traditions are kept alive and continuously renewed, otherwise they would become remnants of a remote past and be a burden, an obstacle.

(2) The main objective is certainly to work together for a living, serving, and witnessing present and future of Christians in the Middle East, in face of the great challenges of emigration, and of integration into the Arab world—inseparably linked to coexistence and dialogue with the Muslim majority. In this sense also, the churches want to promote a real common witness and service in the fields of development, service to the refugees and to the needy, relief in cases of emergency, etc.

(3) The common use of the Arabic language is an important tool to unite most of the churches and Christians of the region, beyond their historical traditions. It is also an indispensable factor for the integration into the surrounding Arab world, or simply for a renewed inculturation. There is a growing interest in drawing inspiration from the ancient Arab Christian literature that flourished, especially between the eighth and thirteenth centuries. However, here also the

results are not always self-evident. For instance, working groups representing the different traditions have labored several years to establish together a common Arabic translation of the Lord's Prayer and the Nicean-Constantinopolitan Creed. A valuable and scientific work was done, but many churches are reluctant to adopt the new texts, because they were afraid that people may look at the slight changes as a break with tradition.

(4) Finally, it must be recognized that the MECC is a very active instrument in promoting formation and active participation of lay people in the life of the churches. As a result, little by little a certain number of problems related to the unity of the churches and future Christian presence in the Middle East may, hopefully, be seen in a different light, and new responses may be found.

Local Collaboration

However, it must be noted that the MECC does not intend to monopolize the ecumenical activities in the region. Besides, the Middle East is not in the least a homogeneous entity. There are not only many different historical traditions in the churches but also deep-rooted and far-reaching differences between countries and regions. This is equally true for ecumenical relations. That is why I would like to end by pointing out some of these local diversities and possibilities.

Antioch

In the traditional territory of the Patriarchate of Antioch, that is to say mainly the present countries of Lebanon and Syria, a concern dear to the Greek Orthodox patriarch Ignatius IV Hazim is to revive a synodical process involving the churches of the region. Without waiting until visible unity can be reached, churches should start meeting and working together on a regular basis, in the social and the pastoral fields. Such a dynamic would bring the churches closer to each other and at the same time would be an empowering factor in difficult tasks.

The most remarkable initiative in this sense is the pastoral agreement between the Greek Orthodox and the Syrian Orthodox patriarchates of Antioch in the year 1991. This agreement provides for collaboration in practically all pastoral and liturgical fields, except for the Eucharistic concelebration and ordination.

Still in the same territory of Antioch, as far back as 1974, meetings took place between the synods of the Greek Orthodox and the Greek Catholic patriarchates in view of re-establishing unity on the local level, without waiting for an agreement on the universal level. New contacts and statements in 1995 and 1996 raised new expectations, however some of them were unrealistic. Both synods clarified their positions and decided to continue to work together and do whatever possible in common, but far from the media and avoiding sensation.

In Jerusalem also there are new reasons for joy and hope because of the new prevailing spirit in inter-church relations and the new forms of collaboration, but we shall have the opportunity to come back to it tomorrow.

Finally, Iraq seems far away from us here and contacts are not easy. However even there, a growing ecumenical collaboration is taking place, especially between the Chaldean and the Assyrian churches, as a first result of the Christological agreement of 1994. For instance, priests of both churches are formed in the same seminary in Baghdad. As late as November 1996, the patriarchs of both churches, Raphael I Bidawid and Mar Denkha IV, signed a joint statement at the end of their first official meeting, in the USA, to discuss prospects of unity between their churches. In this statement they envisaged concrete initiatives to work towards future unity.

On the level of the whole of the Middle East, we should also be aware of the work of the Fellowship of the Middle East Evangelical Churches (FMEEC), bringing together Reformed, Episcopal, and Lutheran churches. At its fourth General Assembly, which was held in Cyprus in March 1997, a document entitled "Proposal for Evangelical Unity in the Middle East" was unanimously accepted. It is the result of three years of study, review, and preparation by the fellowship's Theological Committee. Intended to bring about full fellowship among the Evangelical churches in the region, the text will be sent to all member churches for study and comment. This proposal is seen as a critical step forward and a sign of a new vitality given to the fellowship. For the first time in several years, representatives from Sudan, Iran, and Algeria were able to attend.

Finally, allow me to mention in this context another initiative, although it is not ecumenical in itself, namely the regular meetings of the Council of Catholic patriarchs of the Middle East. It is interesting to note that ecumenism is at its origin. In fact, the first meeting of the Catholic patriarchs of this region took place in Cyprus, during the 1990 General Assembly of the MECC, the first one in which Catholics took part officially. The Council of the Catholic Patriarchs is also ecumenical in its results. This is eloquently illustrated by their meeting in Lebanon, last October. The Greek Orthodox and the Syrian Orthodox patriarchs as well as Armenian Orthodox Catholics took part in their meeting, during the first day. This resulted in a new pastoral agreement between the churches represented, on three points: mixed marriages, a common catechism for government schools, and the practices of first Holy Communion in the Catholic schools. This agreement applies directly only to the territory of Antioch, but it may soon also have repercussions for other countries in the region.

THREE

The Churches in Jerusalem

Frans Bouwen

∞

Jerusalem occupies a unique place in the life of the Church as it does in the Bible and in salvation history. For a Christian, a visit to Jerusalem and to the biblical places cannot be separated from an encounter with the church of Jerusalem, the "living stones" who give life to the historical places, because of the uninterrupted witness of the local Christian community to the resurrection of Christ, on the very places where everything started.

Then immediately the question arises: where is the church of Jerusalem? In fact, the pilgrim or visitor may find himself or herself perplexed in front of the diversity and division of the churches in Jerusalem.

First of all, it is of fundamental importance to distinguish clearly between diversity and division. Such a distinction is not always obvious to a Western visitor who for the first time meets with the churches of Jerusalem, face to face, and especially the Oriental churches.

Diversity is not only legitimate, it is also an enrichment for the Church. The mystery of the revelation of God's love in Christ is so infinitely rich that no language or culture can expect to grasp it fully and even less express it adequately. Each culture approaches this mystery in its own way and discovers and emphasizes in it some specific aspects or affinities. When, in the oneness of the Christian communion, these different approaches and discoveries are brought together in harmony, then we can hope to come to a greater fullness in knowledge, expression and liturgical celebration.

It is to these rich diversities that visitors in Jerusalem are called to be open in the first place. A visit to Jerusalem is really a unique opportunity to learn to appreciate and love such discoveries. It is also an excellent opportunity to experience how the Gospel has gone a long way and reached countless peoples and cultures around the world and how all come to look for renewal and inspiration in this tiny spot.

Unfortunately, this diversity, for many reasons, has become division, also here in Jerusalem. And this division is indeed a great scandal in Jerusalem, even more so because it was in Jerusalem that Jesus lived, preached, prayed, and died for the unity of the children of God. Here, on the first Pentecost, the Holy Spirit brought many peoples and languages together in one proclamation of the Good News and one doxology for God's salvation. Here the first disciples devoted themselves to the Apostles' teaching and fellowship, to the breaking of bread and prayers, being of one heart and soul.

Anyhow, it has to be said immediately: not one of the existing divisions was born here, in Jerusalem. They were all imported here. They originated in different parts of the world and when all the churches wanted to be present in Jerusalem, they brought their divisions with them. As long as these divisions were scattered around the world, in their places of origin, the scandal was less visible. But when all want to come and live in this small spot, the scandal just explodes.

In that sense, the church of Jerusalem is not the only one responsible for these divisions. On the contrary, all our churches contributed to them, in one way or another, and as a consequence, they have their own part of responsibility in it, as well as their own duty to work for unity in Jerusalem.

Churches Present in Jerusalem

When it comes to present briefly the churches that are present in Jerusalem, experience has taught me that the easiest way is not always the most theological one. I usually distinguish the following categories:

(1) First, in Jerusalem we have three patriarchs:

the Greek Orthodox patriarch
the Armenian Apostolic or Orthodox patriarch
the Latin patriarch

It is interesting to note that the term "patriarch" has in each instance a different meaning.

(2) Secondly, there are three Oriental Orthodox archbishops:

the Syrian Orthodox archbishop
the Coptic Orthodox archbishop
the Ethiopian Orthodox archbishop

(3) Thirdly, there are five Oriental Catholic patriarchal vicars, or representatives of Catholic patriarchs who have their residences elsewhere:

the Greek Catholic or Melkite patriarchal vicar
the Maronite patriarchal vicar
the Syrian Catholic patriarchal vicar
the Armenian patriarchal vicar
the Chaldean patriarchal vicar

(4) In the fourth place, there are

the Episcopal or Anglican bishop
the Evangelical Lutheran bishop

Together they constitute the thirteen traditionally recognized churches in Jerusalem and the Holy Land, who signed, together with the Franciscan Custos of the Holy Land, the common Memorandum on Jerusalem, in November 1994.

If we take the framework of the Middle East Council of Churches, namely the four families of churches, we have the following representations:

(1) The Oriental Orthodox family: four churches

 the Armenian Orthodox Church
 the Syrian Orthodox Church
 the Coptic Orthodox Church
 the Ethiopian Orthodox Church

(2) The Eastern Orthodox family:

 the Greek Orthodox Patriarchate of Jerusalem,
 with an important representation of the Russian Orthodox
 and one of the Rumanian Orthodox Church

(3) The Catholic family: five Oriental Catholic Communities and one Latin

 the Latin Patriarchate
 the Greek Catholic Church
 the Maronite Church
 the Syrian Catholic Church
 the Armenian Catholic Church
 the Chaldean Church

(4) The Evangelical and Episcopal family:

 the Episcopal Church (in Jerusalem and the Middle East)
 the Evangelical Lutheran Church (in Jordan)

There are, of course, in Jerusalem a considerable number of other smaller Protestant or Pentecostal communities; some of them constitute the United Christian Council in Israel. I only mention some of them: the Baptist Churches, the Presbyterian Church, the Christian Brethren Assembly, the Church of God, the Church of the Nazarene, several Pentecostal communities, and so on.

History and Perspective

In front of this composite mosaic of churches, is it possible to introduce some perspective? Or are these churches all on the same level? Do they all carry the same weight?

It is rather delicate to answer such questions, since almost every church has its own reading and interpretation of history. The harmonization and reconciliation of these many different histories may be one of the most demanding tasks, if one wants to work for the unity of the church of Jerusalem. I am going to give it a try nevertheless, and I apologize in advance if, unwittingly, in spite of my best efforts, I may hurt the sensitivities of someone among us.

In order to be able to see some perspective in the relations among the churches in Jerusalem, it is absolutely necessary to go back in history.

Since the first Pentecost, a Christian community was present in Jerusalem. From the beginning, this community offered a clear diversity: disciples coming from a Jewish background and others coming from a pagan background; some speaking Aramaic, others Greek.

This diversity increased tremendously with the freedom of Christianity in the Roman Empire under Constantine the Great in the fourth century, and the rapid development of Christian pilgrimages to the Holy Land. Very soon most churches not only came on pilgrimage, but also wanted to have a permanent representation in Jerusalem. In the fourth and the early fifth century, that created no problems. Although of different liturgical traditions, all these churches constituted one church and the local bishop of Jerusalem was considered by all as being their bishop when they came to Jerusalem. This beautiful diversity in unity was also experienced in the many monasteries in the nearby desert.

Unfortunately, this situation changed dramatically as a consequence of the Council of Chalcedon (451). After a prolonged period of tension and unrest, the church of Jerusalem remained united in its reception of Chalcedon; there was no split in the church hierarchy in Jerusalem as happened in Alexandria and Antioch. However the Armenian, Syrian, and Coptic Churches, who refused the Council of Chalcedon, were from then on no longer in communion with the church of Jerusalem. So, when they came to Jerusalem, they no longer recognized the bishop of Jerusalem as their own and, little by little, these pilgrim churches brought their own bishop with them to Jerusalem, thus establishing separate churches. This was the first multiplication of churches in Jerusalem.

A further step in the direction of the creation of another separate community was made at the time of the Crusaders. The Crusaders made one of their bishops Latin patriarch of Jerusalem thinking that by doing so they would reestablish unity between the church of Jerusalem and the church of Rome, forty-five years after the great schism between East and West in 1054. It could appear to be true on the level of the hierarchy, but it never became a reality on the level of the community. In fact it was a rather forced union and created more resentment than communion. Anyhow, this Latin patriarchate had to leave Jerusalem together with the Crusaders.

The Franciscan Friars established themselves in a permanent way in Jerusalem during the fourteenth century, in order to be in charge of the Catholic Holy Places. They erected sanctuaries and started slowly to gather small Catholic communities around them.

Finally, last century brought about a radical change in the fabric of the churches in Jerusalem and gave them their present outlook. In the nineteenth century, for the first time, Western missionaries could enter the Holy Land in greater numbers, with relative freedom. They all wanted to come and offer assistance to the existing churches in Jerusalem, which were then in great need of help, after three centuries under Ottoman rule. Unfortunately, instead of helping the local church to renew itself from within and to acquire a new vitality, almost all these missionaries ended up creating new churches alongside the existing ones: Catholic, Anglican, Lutheran, and other Protestant communities. And these communities were built up not with Jews or Muslims converted to Christianity, but mainly with Orthodox faithful who became Catholic, Anglican, Lutheran, and so on. By saying so, I do not want to judge what happened then, and much less would I dare to condemn the persons who were involved. I only mention what happened. A good hundred years later, in the light of further developments, we can only regret that it has not been possible to proceed differently, and we can understand that this period remains like an open wound for the local Orthodox Church to the present day.

In light of this historical survey, it seems possible to say that there is in Jerusalem a Christian community that is a direct continuation of the church of the Acts of the Apostles, throughout the centuries, in spite of the very difficult circumstances it experienced at times. The language and national belonging of this community may have changed: Aramaic, Greek, Arabic. The leadership or hierarchy of this community may have changed: at times the leadership was local, at times it came from abroad. Nevertheless, the community in itself remained the same, a continuity in the midst of many changes.

Around this local church community, we can discern the presence of what we can call the pilgrim churches, representations in Jerusalem of different home-churches, starting mainly from the fourth century on.

Finally, in the nineteenth century, different missionary churches were added to them, as a result of the arrival of the Western missionaries.

In my opinion, the church that appears to be most entitled to consider itself as the local community in direct continuation with the early church is the Greek Orthodox Church, notwithstanding the fact that its hierarchy is today mainly composed of expatriates. It is the local living community, which for centuries spoke Arabic, that is the main support of this continuity. This is implicitly or de facto recognized by the others by the fact that they all consider the Greek Orthodox patriarch as the first among all heads of churches in Jerusalem. He always presides over their regular meetings and these meetings usually take place in the Greek Orthodox Patriarchate. Around this community we have the pilgrim churches (Armenians, Syrians, Copts, Ethiopians) and then the missionary churches of last century.

When we look at the churches in Jerusalem in this way, new perspectives open up before us. These perspectives help us to understand better the dynamics of the relations between churches and their mutual sensitivities and acceptance.

Ecumenical Relations

These perspectives also make it possible to reach a deeper understanding of ecumenical relations. In fact, two main obstacles inherited from the past continue to weigh heavily on the ecumenical climate in

Jerusalem, namely the problems related to the Holy Places and the repercussions of the creation of the missionary churches of last century as well as the proselytism that went with it.

As is well known, tensions, conflicts, and at times confrontations happened sporadically between the churches during several centuries. The mistrust, isolation, and resentments that resulted were rather the opposite of what we call today ecumenical relations. It takes a long time to change ancient mentalities and attitudes. Nevertheless, it must be said that important progress has been made in this field during the last decades, thanks to the restoration work in the Holy Sepulchre, starting in the 1950s. Since parts of this building are common property while other parts belong to different communities, and since it was threatening to collapse on the heads of all, the churches were compelled to do something about it together. They had to learn how to plan and work together, and so, step by step, they got to know and trust each other. Some may judge that the restoration done is not perfect, especially from the aesthetic point of view, but many things have changed in the course of the years. The best recent illustration of this was the solemn inauguration of the inner decoration of the dome above the tomb of Christ on January 2, 1997. After 20 years of waiting, the scaffolding has finally been removed, something unprecedented has been achieved together. For the first time in history, the three patriarchs of Jerusalem presided over the inauguration ceremony, side by side. A real joy for the church of Jerusalem! However if this celebration was a sign of what had been achieved, it was also a reminder of what still remains to be done. In fact, the three communities prayed one after the other, but were not yet able to pray together. Briefly, it is now possible for the churches to work together within the framework of the "status quo" of 1757 and 1852, but it is not yet possible for them to work together in order to adapt this "status quo" to the present circumstances. More mutual confidence is still needed. This will be one of the great challenges for the year 2000, in view of the many pilgrims to be expected.

The creation of the missionary churches and the question of proselytism that is generally associated with it left, no doubt, even deeper wounds. Their consequences weigh at present more heavily on ecumenical relations. It is a very complex and sensitive issue, with many roots and implications. It arose mainly last century, but does it really belong to the past or is it still a present day issue? It is a fact that, as late as 1989, the Greek Orthodox Patriarchate of Jerusalem announced its withdrawal from the International Theological Dialogue between the Roman Catholic Church and the Orthodox Church, giving as the main reason for his withdrawal that the Catholics exploited the dialogue in order to mislead the Orthodox faithful, making them believe that there were no longer real differences between both churches and attracting them in this way to the Catholic Church. On the other hand, Catholics have genuinely been trying to put into practice the ecumenical orientations of the Second Vatican Council. It takes time to change mentalities and long-time habits. Nevertheless Catholics sincerely believe that their attitudes towards the Orthodox have changed. How is it that the Orthodox do not seem to be entirely convinced of it? It is clear that a number of situations and practices are not seen and evaluated in the same way. On this point especially, much remains to be done in order to come to a better mutual knowledge and a deeper mutual knowledge and a deeper mutual trust. To build up such a trust together seems to be the main task for the churches of Jerusalem in the ecumenical field.

How then can we describe the present state of relations among the churches in Jerusalem? In the course of the last thirty years, they have gradually become more frequent, more spontaneous, more fraternal, and more fruitful.

The pilgrimage of Pope Paul VI, in 1964, and his meetings in Jerusalem with Patriarch Athenagoras of Constantinople and Patriarch Benedictos of Jerusalem opened a new era. At first sight nothing concrete changed immediately, but afterwards nothing remained quite the same. In the course of the following years, there have been slow developments, a few steps forward and at times also a few steps backward.

In my personal opinion, during the last ten years, the difficult general situation has played a very important role, especially the years of the "intifada" or Palestinian uprising. These years were years of suffering and trial, for the churches and for the Christians, a time which put them to the test. Under the pressure of the events and pushed by the laity, the heads of churches were compelled to come together and consult each other, in order to take a common stand and to say a common word on the situation: to call for prayers for peace, to demand respect for human dignity and human rights, to condemn injustice and violence.

In this way, step by step, patriarchs, bishops and other heads of churches acquired the reflex to contact each other, consult, and act together. They discovered that this was not only a vital necessity, but also their deepest desire and a true dimension of this ministry. Somehow it was something that had always been there but that they had been unable to recognize and did not know how to express.

The most tangible result of this rapprochement was the common "Memorandum on the significance of Jerusalem for Christians," signed in common by the heads of the main churches in Jerusalem, in November 1994. Already the mere existence of this memorandum is greatly significant. After centuries of conflict and tension on the question of the Holy Places, the churches in Jerusalem were now able to state together, in one voice, what Jerusalem means to them and what rights, in their view, result from this significance for the churches and their living communities.

Moreover, on the occasion of the signature of this memorandum, the same heads of churches decided that from then on they would have a monthly meeting, under the presidency of the Greek Orthodox Patriarch and in his residence. And since then, they have been faithful to this resolution, by meeting more or less every two months. For Jerusalem, that means an enormous step forward, something that ten years ago most observers would have thought simply impossible, a utopia. True, this progress remains fragile and needs to be consolidated and deepened, but it is a real sign of hope.

If one would like to describe briefly this new kind of collaboration, one could say that the churches in Jerusalem are now able to face the important common issues of the day together. However it remains more difficult to study together the problems that exist between the churches and the complaints one may have against the other, as for example the delicate question of proselytism. But even in this field, some first steps have been taken recently.

The preparations for the celebration of the year 2000 may be another providential opportunity on the way to unity. Coordination and cooperation will be of vital importance for the churches in Jerusalem, if they want to welcome the millions of pilgrims expected for that year. What image of the church of Jerusalem do we want to present to these visitors: an image of mutual ignorance and division? or the image of a church that takes its vocation to unity and its common witness seriously? The creation of a local Ecumenical Commission for the year 2000 is a first step in that direction.

After this description of the relations between the churches on the level of the church authorities, we should not forget the inter-church relations on the level of the lay people.

Generally speaking lay people more spontaneously identify themselves as "Christians" in front of the non-Christian majority, while the clergy would more frequently identify themselves with their confessional community: Greek Orthodox or Greek Catholic, Latin, Maronite, Armenian, etc.

The patterns of relationships are also very different. Almost in every family one can find Catholic and Orthodox members, and also Protestants, as a result of the frequent mixed marriages. Sometimes there is a feeling of a double belonging or a tendency to take part in the life of both churches. In many social, cultural and even religious organizations, men and women of different churches have been working closely together long before the recent ecumenical developments. A growing active participation of these men and women in the life of the churches would certainly strengthen the ecumenical relations and would increase the pressure to come to concrete results.

The most visible expression of the desire for unity on the level of the faithful is their untiring efforts to come to a common date for the celebration of Easter and Christmas. They see it as a sign of Christian credibility and a social expression of their unity in the eyes of the Muslim majority. In several villages the faithful have compelled the pastors to go ahead with common celebrations without asking for official approval. Some concrete actions may be judged differently by the church authorities, but in general such insistence is healthy for the churches.

While clearly maintaining the distinction between ecumenism and inter-religious dialogue, one must recognize that in Jerusalem the inter-religious dialogue plays also a considerable ecumenical role. Christians of many different churches and confessions are involved together in dialogue with Muslims and Jews. Together they reflect on their faith and try to explain it in common, in the presence of their Muslim or Jewish partners. Therefore they are obliged to try to find new terms and new ways of expressing their faith and their life. By doing so some polarizations disappear and new possibilities may be discovered to overcome deadlocks of the past.

Common Tasks and Challenges

Inter-religious dialogue is only one of the many tasks the churches in Jerusalem are called to face together. The main one remains obviously the whole question of a just and durable peace. What is the role of the churches in the peace process? And what can a growing understanding and unity among the churches contribute to the construction of trust and collaboration between the different nationalities and religions in this part of the world?

Other issues related to it are the emigration and constant decreasing proportion of Christians in the total population, the involvement of Christians in the new Palestinian entity that is in preparation, the questions of religion and state in a context where Islam and Judaism do not make the same distinction, and others. There is a need for bringing some church communities home to the Middle East of today. Those communities that were founded by expatriate missionaries sometimes felt more at home in the expatriate culture than in their own Palestinian or Arabic surroundings. What does it mean to be a church in a situation of conflict, when a new nation is in the making, and when the whole Middle East is on the threshold of profound changes in inter-religious and inter-state relations? How can a Christian be personally involved in this political turmoil and by so doing be inspired by his or her faith, rooted in tradition but facing the future in hope? These are some of the questions that will have to be answered.

Conclusion

Allow me to conclude by going back to a question I raised in the beginning. I have been speaking not only of the churches in Jerusalem, but also of the church of Jerusalem. Where is that church of Jerusalem to be found?

Is it in the many international representations or buildings, biblical institutes, theological faculties, hostels for pilgrims, monasteries with members coming from all over the world? These institutions give a rather foreign image to the church in Jerusalem and seem to attract the main attention of the worldwide church to themselves.

Or does the church of Jerusalem mainly rest upon the small local Christian community that has been living here for centuries? These Christians for whom Jerusalem is not only a holy city, but is a city like any other, because it is the place where they were born and where they are at home. At times these local Christians have the feeling of being ignored by the visitors and by the worldwide church. They would like to have a greater say in the life of church institutions, would like to see their own language used more frequently. They sometimes feel like telling those visitors: leave us some room to be ourselves, to find and develop our own identity, so that we may receive you as our guests.

However such questions may confuse you even more, and I was asked to introduce you to the churches in Jerusalem and not to confuse you. So it is better to stop here. At least I hope that you agree with me that the church of Jerusalem is alive. As a small minority its future is never entirely secure, humanly speaking, but it offers a living and unbroken witness to the death and resurrection of Christ in the places where it all happened. This Jerusalem church is ready to share its unique experience with all the incoming pilgrims, while at the same time it counts on the worldwide church, for loving communion and fraternal support, in order to be able to continue its service and witness, both to the local society and to the world at large.

FOUR

Ecumenical Education and Formation: An Urgent Need for Further Progress in Ecumenical and Interfaith Relations

Cardinal Edward Idris Cassidy

∞

A first premise of the following reflections is that there is great need for progress in ecumenical as well as in interfaith relations, and this for the sake of humankind. The second premise is that ecumenical relations are different from interfaith relations in spite of the confusion which often exists in the use of these terms. Their starting point is different, and so are their aims. Yet part of their dynamics are quite similar and ultimately they do have a common goal, i.e., the unity and wholeness of humankind. As Pope John Paul II wrote in *Ut Unum Sint,* his encyclical letter on commitment to ecumenism, "the unity of all divided humanity is the will of God" (*UUS,* 6).

The Second Vatican Council's Decree on Ecumenism, *Unitatis Redintegratio,* reflecting on "the sacred mystery of the unity of the Church," referred to the Church as "a sacrament of the unity of all mankind" (cf. *Lumen Gentium,* 1), "God's only flock, like a standard lifted high for the nations to see, [ministering] the gospel of peace to all mankind" (*UR,* 2). And the council stated in its Declaration on the Relationship of the

Church to Non-Christian Religions, *Nostra Aetate,* that "in her task of fostering unity and love among men, and even among nations, [the Church] gives primary consideration [in this document] to what human beings have in common and to what promotes fellowship among them," for "all people comprise a single community, and have a single origin, since God made the whole race of men dwell over the entire face of the earth (cf. Acts 17:26). One also is their final goal: God" (*NA,* 1).

If it is true, as we believe it is, that the Church is to be "a sacrament of the unity of all mankind" (*LG,* 1), i.e., both signifying it and bringing it about, then the Church's commitment to engage in ecumenical as well as in interfaith relations is a vital part of the process.

Pope John Paul II has reflected on this in the first chapter of *Ut Unum Sint,* putting it in the realm of God's plan with his Church and with the world. In this chapter, centered on the Church's commitment to ecumenism, the Holy Father quotes from a *Letter to the Bishops of the Catholic Church on Some Aspects of the Church Understood as Communion,* published by the Congregation for the Doctrine of the Faith in May 1992:

> Together with all Christ's disciples, the Catholic Church bases upon God's plan her ecumenical commitment to gather all Christians into unity. Indeed, "the Church is not a reality closed in on herself. Rather, she is permanently open to missionary and ecumenical endeavour, for she is sent to the world to announce and witness, to make present and spread the mystery of communion which is essential to her, and to gather all people and all things into Christ, so as to be for all an 'inseparable sacrament of unity'"—the unity of all divided humanity is the will of God.

It is for this reason that God sent his Son (*UUS,* 6) who through the cross, as the Letter of Saint Paul to the Ephesians explains, "broke down the dividing wall of hostility" (2:14–16). And the Holy Father continues his reflection:

> On the eve of his sacrifice on the Cross, Jesus himself prayed to the Father for his disciples and for all those who believe in him, that

they might be one, a living communion. This is the basis not only of the duty, but also of the responsibility before God and his plan, which falls to those who through Baptism become members of the Body of Christ, a Body in which the fullness of reconciliation and communion must be made present. (*UUS*, 6)

To be *present* in this way is the calling of the Church in a world that lives pretty much on the fringe of *absence*. Our cities are full of marginalization and loneliness. Our society is run on the basis of consumption. Our youngsters feel confused, frustrated, and empty. All these conditions are so many causes of fear, and if you come to think of it, everything we fear, and indeed fear itself, occurs on the fringe of absence. Was this not what the disciples of Jesus were feeling when without warning a violent storm came up on the lake, and their boat began to be swamped by the waves? Jesus was asleep. To the disciples he was on the fringe of absence, so they woke him up saying, "Lord, save us! We are lost" (cf. Matt. 8:24–26), thus making him "present" to them again. And presence became salvation. Jesus stood up and took the winds and the sea to task. Complete calm ensued.

In today's world many people are at a loss too. But "Where are you?" God asks them, as he asked Adam and Eve in the Bible (Gen. 3:9). God makes himself present to them, enters into communion with them. The Incarnation of his Son is the most significant event which ever happened in human history, and it is the mission of the Church to witness effectively to its truth. Her presence, therefore, should not be divided just as her Lord through whom God gave her the ministry of reconciliation is not divided (cf. 1 Cor. 1:13; 2 Cor. 5:18).

Reconciliation, healing, wholeness are so much needed in a world which is suffering the consequences of both its mistakes and its achievements. The potential of technology to build as well as to destroy is an illustration of this. Outer space has become part of man's domain, but with it comes also the awareness that mother earth has become a fragile little planet suspended in the universe. Through this awareness, humankind has gained not only a strong sense of interdependence but also of vulnerability. Faced with this reality some of our young people try to ignore it or to get out of it. Others though try to relate to it. They try to understand what it really means to be human, and to be human *together*. They wish to be the architects of their own future, anticipating the problems and beginning the design of the solutions. In this process religion can play and often does play an important role (but unfortunately pseudo-religions do too). I would like to quote from Vatican II's Declaration *Nostra Aetate:*

> Men look to the various religions for answers to those profound mysteries of the human condition which, today even as in olden times, deeply stir the human heart: What is a man? What is the meaning and the purpose of our life? What is goodness and what is sin? What gives rise to our sorrows and to what intent? Where lies the path to true happiness? What is the truth about death, judgement, and retribution beyond the grave? What, finally, is that ultimate and unutterable mystery which engulfs our being, and whence we take our rise, and whither our journey leads us? (*NA,* 1)

Do these fundamental questions not call for a credible response, and therefore for urgent intensification of ecumenical endeavours within the Christian family, as well as of dialogue between all people who have what *Nostra Aetate* describes as "a certain perception of that hidden power which hovers over the cause of things and over the events of human life?" (*NA,* 2).

With regard to ecumenism, this core of the quest for the restoration of unity among all Christians, which was a chief concern of Vatican II, is imperative for all of us Christians. The Pope has expressed this beautifully in *Ut Unum Sint:*

> Jesus himself, at the hour of his Passion, prayed "that they may all be one" (John 17:21). This unity, which the Lord has bestowed on his Church and in which he wishes to embrace all people, is not something added on, but stands at the very heart of Christ's mission. Nor is it some secondary attribute of the community of his disciples. Rather, it belongs to the very essence of this community. *God wills the Church, because he wills unity,* and unity is an expression of the whole depth of his *agape.* (*UUS,* 9)

I think that we are being challenged by these words. I hope we are. Vatican II affirmed that "concern for restoring unity pertains to the whole Church, faithful and clergy alike," that "it extends to everyone" (*UR*, 5). Yet, thirty years after the close of the Council (and I am borrowing words of Pope Pius XII, in an address to the Italian Youth in 1958), too many Christians "are not at all awakening to the sudden flowering of the unexpected spring" caused by the Holy Spirit. This lack of understanding the urgency of the ecumenical imperative, the urgency of the unity of the Church for the sake of the unity of humankind, is mainly due to a lack of ecumenical education and formation. The same is true as far as the need for interreligious dialogue is concerned. One needs to learn to look with respect upon the religious beliefs and convictions of others and the ways of conduct inspired by them. One needs to learn about discerning, acknowledging, and even promoting the spiritual and moral riches found in their religion, and the values found in their culture (cf. *NA*, 2). But as the interest and involvement in ecumenical and interfaith dialogue needs learning, this learning also needs nurturing. It is an ongoing process.

Pope John Paul II has often spoken and written about dialogue. His personalist approach helps us discover similarities in the dynamics of ecumenical dialogue and interfaith dialogue. At the same time he points to the essential aspects that our educational programs ought to take into account in this regard.

> The capacity for "dialogue" is rooted in the nature of the person and his dignity. . . . Dialogue is an indispensable step along the path *towards human self-realization,* the self-realization both of *each individual* and *of every human community.* Although the concept of "dialogue" might appear to give priority to the cognitive dimension (*dia-logos*), all dialogue implies a global, existential dimension. It involves the human subject in his or her entirety; dialogue between communities involves in a particular way the subjectivity of each. . . . Dialogue is not simply an exchange of ideas. In some way it is always an "exchange of gifts." (*UUS*, 28)

For this reason the Pope emphasizes the importance of mutual respect and sensitivity, in fairness and truth, as necessary preconditions for engaging in dialogue. This concern must therefore guide the way in which we design our educational programs. In fact, these programs should not merely be suitable to the particular destiny of the individuals, but they should also be conducive to "fraternal relations with others," "in order to promote true unity and peace in the world."[1]

Pope Pius XII had already spoken along these lines in 1952: "The direction which society will take tomorrow will be largely decided by the mind and heart of university students of today." [2] The heart and the mind, the affective as well as the cognitive are essential components of our Catholic understanding of education. This holistic understanding is also an underlying factor in a study document on ecumenical formation published in May 1993 by the Joint Working Group between the Catholic Church and the World Council of Churches:

> The very dynamic of ecumenism is relational in character. We respond in faith and hope to God who relates to us in love, commanding us to love one another (Mark 12:29–31). This response ought to be "wholehearted." Therefore, in order to help Christians to respond wholeheartedly to the ecumenical imperative, we must seek ways to relate the prayer of Jesus (John 17:20–24) to all our hearts and minds, to the affective as well as to the cognitive dimensions in them. Christians must be helped to understand that to love Jesus necessarily means to love everything Jesus prayed, lived, died and was raised for, namely "to gather into one the children of God who are scattered abroad" (John 11:52), the unity of his disciples as an effective sign of the unity of all peoples.[3]

Another feature of ecumenical formation is the actual involvement in dialogue experience, individually and in community. God speaks to us today the words which he addressed to Cain: "Where is your brother?" (Gen. 4:9). As the Joint Working Group's study document states: "All Christians should become aware, and make each other aware, of who and where their sisters and brothers are and where they stand in regard to them, whether near or far (Eph. 2:17). They should be helped to go out to meet them, to get involved with them. Involvement and participation in the whole ecumenical foundation process is crucial." Moreover, the study document affirms, "in a Christian response to God and the ecumenical imperative which comes from God, there is no such thing as 'the few for the many.' The response to the prayer of Jesus must be the response of each and every one. There-fore, the growth into an ecumenical mind and heart is essential for each and for all, and the introduction of, and care for, ecumenical for-mation are absolutely necessary at every level of the church commu-nity, church life, action and activities; at all educational levels." And, the document goes on to say, "while ecumenical formation must be an essential feature in every curriculum in theological training, care must be taken that it does not become something intended for individuals only. There must be a commitment to learning in community."

We also need to emphasize, as the above-mentioned study docu-ment of the Joint Working Group does, that commitment to ecumeni-cal dialogue—and this is *mutatis mutandis* especially true with re-gard to interreligious dialogue—does not at all imply to gloss over existing differences, nor to deny the specific profiles of our respective traditions. However, it may involve a common re-reading of our his-tories, and especially of those events that led to divisions, tensions, hostility. "It is not enough to regret that our histories have been tainted through the polemics of the past," the Joint Working Group's docu-ment says, "ecumenical formation must endeavour to eliminate po-lemic and to further mutual understanding, reconciliation and the healing of memories." In the words of Saint Paul, no longer shall we be strangers to one another but members of the one household of God (Eph. 2:19).

It is at this point in its explanation of what ecumenical formation means and how it ought to be realized that the study document calls for openness to other religions as an integral part of the ecumenical education and formation process, underlining the difference between ecumenism and interreligious dialogue:

> In this world, people are also divided along religious lines. Thus ecumenical formation must also address the matter of religious plurality and secularism, and inform about interreligious dialogue which aims at deeper mutual understanding in the search for world community. It must be clear however that interreligious dialogue—with other world religions such as Islam, Buddhism, Hinduism, etc.—has goals that are specifically different from the goals of ecu-menical dialogue among Christians.

This spirit of openness should not remain a characteristic of a "chosen few." It "must get to the pews and market places where people feel the strains of the different heritages which encounter each other." Moreover, the belief that God is the Creator and Sustainer of all also requires from us to do everything in our power to promote the cause of freedom, human rights, justice and peace everywhere. Good relations between people of different faiths and faith traditions can contribute positively to a movement of human solidarity in obedience to God's will.

Ecumenical education and formation is indeed urgently needed if we want to make any significant progress in this. In fact, the world is a "global village" in which peoples, cultures and religions, and indeed other Christian traditions, which were once far off, are now next door to one another. The sense of the "other" is being pressed on all of us, and we *need* to relate to one another if it were only for the very sake of mutual survival. However, there is a deeper reason for the need to relate to others in ecumenical and interfaith dialogue. We find this reason in our very Christian nature and mission. In the words of Pope John Paul II's apostolic letter *Tertio Millennio Adveniente,* in Jesus Christ, God not only speaks to man but also seeks him out. "It is a search which begins in the heart of God." In fact, if God goes in search of man, He does so because He loves him (cf. *TMA,* 7), wanting to fully reveal man to Himself (cf. *Gaudium et Spes,* 22), enabling him to be a son and to have the dignity of a son. It is therefore the task of the Church, "expert in humanity," to be an effective witness to this by communicating her "expertise" to everyone else, starting with her own members.[4] In this regard *education* is of the utmost importance. It prepares people, especially young people, of different faiths and faith traditions to make new discoveries about each other, particularly about each other's faith and tradition, and to discover new possibilities to relate to each other in solidarity and in *truth.*

For instance, the Apostolic Constitution on Catholic Universities, *Ex Corde Ecclesiae,* promulgated by Pope John Paul II in August 1990, bases an important part of its inspiration on those pillars that are also the pillars of ecumenical and interreligious dialogue: the love of truth, the service to human dignity. Expressions such as "knowledge is meant to serve the human person," "the primacy of the person over things," "transcendence of the human person over the world," "the whole development of the person," etc., occur again and again, and are these not amongst the key issues in our world today? More specifically *Ex Corde Ecclesiae* calls on our universities to engage in research that will "seek to discover the roots and causes of the serious problems of our time, paying special attention to their ethical and religious dimensions" (n. 32).

With regard to the formation of the future leadership in the Church, the updated *Directory for the Application of Principles and Norms on Ecumenism*, published by the Pontifical Council for Promoting Christian Unity in March 1993, has dedicated a chapter on the necessity, purpose, means, settings, and content of ecumenical formation. And as far as the preparation of future priests to interfaith dialogue is concerned, Vatican II's Decree *Optatam Totius* requires not only that students "be prepared to enter into dialogue with their contemporaries," but that they "be introduced to a knowledge of other religions" as well. "In general," the Decree on the training of priests goes on to say, "those aptitudes should be cultivated in the students which are most conducive to dialogue. . . . They include the willingness to listen to others and the capacity to open their hearts in a spirit of charity to the various needs of their fellow men" (nn. 15, 16, 17, 19).

A similar vision underlies our understanding of the role of the Catholic school, which "does not exacerbate differences, but rather aids cooperation and contact with others. It opens itself to others and respects their way of thinking and living. It wants to share their anxieties and their hopes as it, indeed, shares their present and future lot in this world."[5]

By way of conclusion, I would like to quote again from our Joint Working Group's study document on ecumenical formation because it summarizes well our topic. "Ecumenism is not an option for the churches," it says. "In obedience to Christ and for the sake of the world the churches are called to be an effective sign of God's presence and compassion before all the nations. For the churches to come divided to a broken world is to undermine their credibility when they claim to have a ministry of universal unity and reconciliation. The ecumenical imperative must be heard and responded to everywhere. This response necessarily requires ecumenical formation which will help the people of God to render a common witness to all humankind by pointing to the vision of the new heaven and a new earth" (Rev. 21:1).

Notes

1. Cf. Vatican II's Declaration on Christian Education, *Gravissimum Educationis,* preface and §§1 and 5.

2. In an address to the Academic Senate of the University of Rome on 15 June 1952.

3. Cf. the "Pontifical Council for Promoting Christian Unity," *Information Service* 84 (1993/III–IV), 176–80.

4. "Apostolic Constitution on Catholic Universities," *Ex Corde Ecclesiae,* n. 3.

5. *The Catholic School,* published in 1977 by the Congregation for Catholic Education. Cf. Remi Hoeckman, "The Role of the Catholic University in the Evangelization of Culture," *Seminarium* 4 (1990), 687–98; "The Teaching on Jews and Judaism in Catholic Education," *Seminarium* 2 (1992), 346–59.

FIVE

The Present Status of the Ecumenical Movement

Anna-Marie Aagaard

∞

The ecumenical movement is approaching its centenary. It has acquired a long history, and only the willfully blind can deny its lasting impact on many churches. Both outside and inside the ecumenical network there is, however, a growing sense that the movement is showing signs of weakness and will need revitalization in order to meet the challenges of a new millennium.

Some react to this perception by calling for a more effective use of the established ecumenical instrumentalities. The ecumenical commitment, not the ecumenical institutions, is ailing, so why make the innocent structures suffer for the non-committed guilty churches?

Current attempts to refocus the ecumenical institutions and lighten the expensive burden of too numerous and too cumbersome structures are, however, also met with some skepticism, because proposals for changes seem disconcerting to people with a long history of investment in the present structures. Putting fresh emphasis on the World Council of Churches' (WCC) role as a catalyst of fellowship, engaging *the member churches* in their ecumenical calling is, for example, perceived as too "church-centered" by those who understand both the WCC and many of the present ecumenical institutions primarily as program agencies or as platforms from which it is possible to talk to or talk at the churches.

The coming assembly (1998) might keep the WCC's structures largely unchanged—with the result that the problem we are facing in the ecumenical movement will not be dealt with in this forum. The problem is both institutional and theological.

The ecumenical movement has to a large extent adopted institutional forms from the secular world. We use parliamentary models for decision making and running meetings of all kinds. We talk of Christian "groups and movements" in the same way that we talk about various political and social initiatives and pressure groups. Concerns for participation and demands for fixed quotas of representation of confessions, regions, women, and youth have only furthered the institutional captivity of ecumenical bodies.[1]

We have, in short, largely agreed to relate to one another according to a political logic. We use the word "council" and borrow it from the early church, but we have avoided the challenge to construct a new logic of Christian life together—new forms of community within which churches may discover the meaning of the one story by which they live and attend together to a distinct way of living in the world. We have no organizational models which adequately will serve "the churches together" in their obedience to Christ's call.

Another response to the felt need for a course-correction calls for a "next ecumenical movement" (S. Mark Heim).[2] The next ecumenical movement will need to create *new* instruments for reaching churches and Christian groups so far unreached by the established councils in order to engage the whole spectrum of the Christian community in at least speaking with one another across the divides of confessional, theological, and cultural traditions.

Continued reliance on present structures and assumptions cannot keep Christian unity at the center of our common calling for two reasons, Heim argues. The tents of the traditional ecumenical institutions are too small. Too small to be a "forum for regular interchange, on a full and equal basis, between Roman Catholic, Pentecostal, Orthodox, evangelical and ecumenical Protestant, independent and indigenous churches." The very large Zionist Christian Church in Southern Africa, an independent church with a membership of mostly poor blacks, is, for example, not yet a part of any structured ecumenical conversation.

A transformation of the present ecumenical movement is also needed because of the real conflicts about moral issues which presently tear Christians apart. Almost a century of trials and errors has taught the churches to address historical confessional differences over creeds, christology, sacraments, and ministry. It has even helped some churches to reconcile such theological differences. A next ecumenical movement must devise new methodologies and new means to address potentially divisive moral issues. Says Heim, "Differences over the nature of other religions, economics, poverty, racial relations, the public status of religion, sexuality, abortion, euthanasia, the role of government: these are today the moral equivalents of denominational differences."

Keep the structures. Make the tents larger. These very different reactions to a sense that the present ecumenical movement needs correction have at least some common ground. They presuppose that the search for Christian unity (however it will be manifested) is the rationale of the ecumenical movement, further, that the deep divisions are the agenda that brings us together.

The conviction suggests that the ecumenical movement moves by climbing a ladder, step by step, until the churches approach a *vision* of Christian unity and spell this vision out in consecutive and ever-refined *models* of unity. They will endeavour to agree on the *forms* of common life and to reach consensus on both the necessary and "the not strictly necessary, but normally normative *norms*" (Michael Root) of common life. The steps of the ladder may become more numerous as new divisions emerge—as at present over a host of moral issues—but the ecumenical trajectory remains: it begins with the status quo of divisions in doctrine and ethos and moves towards the realization of a vision by means of seeking convergences and articulating agreements.

I neither doubt, nor deny, that the "ladder" image applies to a predominant understanding of the ecumenical movement. But the dilemmas it poses are at least beginning to emerge. I shall mention only three which are closely connected:

(1) The nature of "togetherness"

In 1991 the WCC Canberra Assembly adopted a statement named "The Unity of the Church as Koinonia: Gift and Calling." In the encyclical *Ut Unum Sint* Pope John Paul II refers to this statement as an indicator of "the stage we have now reached" in the ecumenical movement. The Canberra statement lists the marks of the unity of the Church as

- a common confession of the apostolic faith;
- a common sacramental life entered by the one baptism and celebrated together in one eucharistic fellowship;
- a common life in which members and ministries are mutually recognized and reconciled;
- and a common mission witnessing to all people the gospel of God's grace and serving the whole of creation" (2.1).

The dilemma of the present ecumenical movement is neither rooted in this or in earlier formulations of the vision, nor in the understanding of Christian unity as both God's "gift" and "calling." The problem arises from the fact that even churches with a common vision and a proven commitment to make it materialize have widely differing theological assumptions regarding the "togetherness" that makes it possible to achieve a *common* vision and the *common* steps towards this vision as realities, and not just as paper tigers.

Some churches take joint engagements in mission and diakonia and joint declarations on matters of faith and order to be in themselves expressions of an existing communio in Christ.

The Porvoo Declaration (1992) of the Anglican and Lutheran churches in Northern Europe commits the churches to "nurture growth in communion" in various, very concrete ways. The "togetherness" of these churches is based on a recognition of "one another's churches as churches belonging to the One, Holy, Catholic and Apostolic Church of Jesus Christ and truly participating in the apostolic mission of the whole people of God" (Declaration a, I).

Even where a eucharistic communion has not yet been possible, there may be a recognition of a real, though imperfect, communion between churches. The lifting of anathemas and the ongoing conversations between the Roman Catholic and the Orthodox churches, may still not be a "togetherness" that embodies the "one fully committed fellowship" (New Delhi), but they are not nothing either. They are signs that the churches recognize each other as "Sister Churches, responsible *together* [my italics] for maintaining the Church of God in fidelity to the divine purpose, most especially in what concerns . . . the search for perfect and total communion" (Balamand 1993).

It becomes much more difficult to articulate the meaning of "togetherness," when the word "church" is used either as a multi-scale concept (from a particular point of view some churches are "more church" than others) or as a concept with widely different meanings. The 1997 "final proposal" for a "Joint Declaration on the Doctrine of Justification" intends to show that "the subscribing Lutheran churches and the Roman Catholic Church are now able to articulate a common understanding of our justification by God's grace through faith in Christ" (5). This sentence is accompanied by a footnote, saying, "The word 'church' is used in this Declaration to reflect the self-understandings of the participating churches, without intending to resolve all the ecclesiological issues related to this term." The footnote makes it possible to interpret the common understanding of justification as a sign of an already existing, real, but imperfect communion, but it also makes it possible to see the "togetherness," expressed in this and in previous bilateral dialogues, as merely instrumental for some future unity in the one Church of Christ.

These examples must suffice to illustrate that the fact of "togetherness" in the ecumenical movement is being interpreted quite differently. The ecumenical movement may be a unity movement, based on a given and embodied unity; on a given and at least partly embodied unity, or it may be a unity movement without any unity. There is no agreement on a language that will interpret the "togetherness." Unless "togetherness" simply refers to a sense that the ecumenical movement in its present stage has reached what was desired, namely friendly coexistence and permeable borders between denominational churches so that individual movements across these borders will be less frowned upon. In that case the ecumenical movement merely means "getting rid of certain uncomfortables" for people who in Western societies constantly are on the move.[3]

(2) The Toronto Statement—and beyond

The Toronto Statement (1950) on "The Church, the churches and the World Council of Churches" still regulates the 'togetherness' in the particular fellowship of churches named the World Council of Churches. Some member churches understand their fellowship in the Council to imply "that . . . a degree of what the New Testament calls *koinonia* [fellowship] already exists. . . [Others] would want to keep an essentially instrumental understanding of the 'fellowship of Churches,' focusing on cooperation and mutual support" (CUV, 33).[4]

The Toronto Statement itself makes neither understanding of the "fellowship of churches" mandatory. Section IV. 4 opens membership in the World Council both to churches which recognize each other as churches and to churches which do not. The particular fellowship in the World Council may be interpreted as a communio-fellowship; as a "broken or incomplete communio"-fellowship, or as a merely instrumental fellowship for which another word may as well be an association. The member churches do not agree in their theological assessment, and it implies that the "ladder" of ecumenical togetherness and the goal of Christian unity, spelt out in unity statements, may be perceived as totally unconnected. The "fellowship" in the WCC is not necessarily considered a part of, or an embodiment of, the goal. The vision has no necessary basis in experience.

The Orthodox churches have, in general, understood the Toronto Statement as a safeguard against Protestant imperialism within the WCC and a *conditio sine qua non* for their participation. Orthodox voices also warn most emphatically against secularizing the "fellowship" and turning both the ecumenical movement and the WCC into totally secular entities.[5] Metropolitan John of Pergamon insists that "the ecclesiological pluralism proposed by the Toronto Statement will have to be rejected. The WCC must . . . eventually acquire a basically common idea of the Church. We cannot go on forever and ever holding different or contradictory views of the Church. It was wise to begin with the ecclesiological *laissez-faire* of Toronto but it would be catastrophic to end with it."

For John of Pergamon it follows that we must distinguish between the WCC being a Church (which it is not) and bearing ecclesiological significance:

Anything that contributes to the building up of the Church or to the reception and fulfillment of the Church's life and unity bears ecclesiological significance. . . .

It is a fact that the Orthodox member churches also most recently have reiterated an instrumental understanding of the WCC as a mere tool for inter-church cooperation and a platform for theological dialogue.[6] It is also a fact that at least some Orthodox theologians will argue that the fellowship of churches within the WCC is not quite nothing. It has "significance" for the unity we seek, and John of Pergamon calls for further reflection that will define the nature of this "significance."

Neither the ecumenical movement in general, nor the WCC in particular, is, however, anywhere near an agreement on the theological vocabulary needed for defining the meaning of the "togetherness in the ecumenical movement" and the "fellowship" in the World Council. It may therefore be wise to listen to Visser't Hooft:

> Let us continue in fellowship, without too much self-consciousness which might become an occasion for pride. It is better to live with a reality which transcends definition than to live with a definition which claims more substance than exists. (CC Report 1963, 138)

The current attempts to arrive at a "Common Understanding and Vision of the World Council of Churches" do not presume to define the nature of this fellowship. A key paragraph of the "Working Draft" puts the weight on an experienced fellowship:

> The essence of the Council is the relationship of the churches to one another. The Council *is* the churches together in fellowship on way towards visible unity. It *has* a structure and organization in order to serve as an instrument for the churches as they work towards *koinonia* in faith, life and witness. (3.4.2)

My reading of the document is that it attempts to turn the discussion about the churches' "togetherness" or "fellowship" 180 degrees around.

The "Working Draft" does not begin with a goal and a ladder and try to reconcile the theological understandings of the relation between the goal and the ladder in a definition of the nature of the "togetherness." The document begins with the undeniable, while experienced, facts of "togetherness" in very concrete acts of worship, witness and service. These facts of common life, listed in the long paragraph 3.6, *describe* a dynamic relational reality. They do *not define* this reality in a conceptual theological language.

Will such a change of perspective make a difference? It will give priority to what the *churches* themselves do or fail to do in their life with each other, and take the emphasis away from what some ecumenical experts "out there" and far away may come up with as the next desired step on the ladder.

An example: Christians of various traditions do worship God together, pray together, and read the Bible together. People assemble; they sing and acknowledge in prayer to be before God. They read from the Bible. They speak of the meaning of the readings and the meaning of the gathering, and they pray for the churches and a world in need. Heaps of worship material testify to the reality of common worship—to the coming before God together. But no one has to my knowledge bothered to study this local material and lift up what the gathered Christians, in Jerusalem, in Wales, or in Johannesburg, in worship together affirm about their faith in God, the Father, Son, and Holy Spirit; about God's gifts and the kingdom; about their togetherness and their readings of Bible, community, and the world. The reality is there, but unexamined, and we do not know how this local worship confirms or critiques the inherited traditions. We have been busy theologizing about the divisions and what *ought to come* at the end of the ladder. If we begin focusing on what is there, not only will a course correction of the ecumenical movement follow, but deepening and widening of the "togetherness" may, just may, also follow.

(3) The one ecumenical movement—the varying principles of ecumenism
The expression "the one ecumenical movement" is today used as a bland reference to ecumenical endeavors all over the world. The ecumenical movement has no privileged center. It is polycentric, and the agents are many—from Latin American Evangelical churches and Pen-

tecostal churches in the U.S. to the Middle East Council of Churches and the Vatican. I recall only one serious discussion about the meaning of the phrase "the one ecumenical movement." Is there *one* ecumenical movement? or two, three, or many?

The expression "the one ecumenical movement" is used in the Joint Working Group's (JWG) First Report, 1966: "Even if there exist in the various churches different ecclesiological principles that govern ecumenical action, we are convinced that the Ecumenical Movement is one and common to all."[7] Before this first "official" appearance the phrase was used by Thomas F. Stransky in his commentary on Vatican II's *De Oecumenismo*.[8] It reflects the change of vocabulary during Vatican II from "Principles of Catholic Ecumenism" to "Catholic Principles of Ecumenism." A restoration of the unity of the Church needs "one single movement" and not many ecumenical movements, stamped respectively "for Catholics only," for "Methodists only," or for "Armenians only."[9]

In this original sense the expression "the one ecumenical movement" is used in the WCC's "Working Draft" (3.14). But how does not interpret the present proliferation of confessional "principles of ecumenism"—these "principles of ecumenism" which traditions bring to bear on the ecumenical movement, and ultimately on the unity we seek?

In *Ut Unum Sint* Pope John Paul II refers to areas needing fuller study before a true consensus of faith can be achieved, namely the relationship between Scripture and Tradition; the understanding of the Eucharist and of ordination; the magisterium of the Church including the ministry of the Bishop of Rome. All these topics have the status of church dividing issues. Consequently they have been, and are, on the agenda of the theological dialogues. A further point is added by the Pope regarding "the Virgin Mary, as Mother of God and Icon of the Church, the spiritual Mother who intercedes for Christ's disciples and for all humanity." Do we have to understand the Pope to mean that the "Catholic principles of ecumenism" now include the understanding of Mary as the Icon of the Church and that unity in faith will require consensus on this particular theological interpretation of Mary?

Do we have to understand the Orthodox Chambésy document of 1995 to mean that the "Orthodox principles of ecumenism" now include not only a firm "no" to women's ordination to priesthood, but also a "no" to abortion and inclusive language when referring to God?

We may say that the ecumenical movement is one, but does the accumulation of confessional principles of ecumenism in reality make it many, because principles are principles and cannot be reinterpreted, let alone sacrificed? And when is enough enough? More than a decade ago some participants in the ecumenical discussion began to ask: What are the *sufficient* principles or preconditions for restoring unity, and what may be left to a future consensus in faith, order, and ethos?[10] Such questions are not new. The Lutheran Reformation declared, "For it is sufficient for the true unity of the Christian church that the gospel be preached in conformity with a pure understanding of it and that the sacraments be administered in accordance with the divine Word" (*Augsburg Confession* VII). Enough is repeatedly said to be enough, but enough is obviously never enough, and never will be enough, as long as we have a static understanding of the unity of the Church and perceive it as an agreement in ideas standing, fixed, on the top of a ladder. Enough will never be enough, as long as we fail to acknowledge that Christian unity can only be given some content through community, through the dynamic inter-relations of the faith communities themselves. Unity is first celebrated, first prayed for, and first lived in bodily actions, before it can be ideally imagined. Unless it reflects upon a practice, ecumenical theology becomes empty. It has nothing to think about.

The most troublesome divide within the ecumenical movement has been, and in my judgment still is, the divide between the parallel histories of Faith and Order, and Life and Work—the two movements out of which the proposals for forming a World Council of Churches grew. The efforts to articulate the nature and unity of the Church and the concentration on practical discipleship have been linked at various points in the history of the ecumenical movement.[11] The conflicts over the apartheid regime in South Africa, for example, fostered an awareness that fundamental ethical issues challenge both the identity of the church and the ecumenical fellowship.

The old divide between Faith and Order concerns and Life and Work concerns has reasserted itself, however, time and again, with most attempts to build a bridge between ecclesiology and ethics producing more questions than answers.

(1) Ecumenical social ethics

It would be only naive to suggest any simple explanation for this impasse, but one element of ecumenical history is at least worth mentioning.

Current research on the history of ecumenical social thought and action reveals that ecumenical social ethics predominantly has been "political ethics."[12] It has been concerned with reducing damages to life so that a greater fullness of life might be achieved. The analyses may have been influenced by biblical visions and the ethical discourse of the various ecclesial traditions, but both the damages to life and the suggested remedies have been posited within the political sphere.

The research lists, in chronological order, the following foci of ecumenical social ethics:

In the years following the Second World War there was an emphasis on freedom and the reduction of social and political constraints of freedom through the protection of human and civil rights. In the context of the cold war a preferential option for reconciliation made churches focus on reducing insecurity through international systems of common security and mutual recognition. Linked with these concerns there was an emphasis on reduction of physical violence through demilitarization and "peace-enforcing." From its very beginning this position failed to gain credibility. There was no consistent ecumenical challenging of selective justifications of warfare.

From the 1960s and onwards ecumenical social ethics turned to reduction of social misery through economic and social participation. Analyses of society made it obvious that racial injustice could not be separated from economic justice, and Bible studies helped to ground endeavors to reduce economic misery in God's preferential option for the poor.

Yet another political indicator for the fullness of life was introduced in the 1970s, namely the reduction of the destruction of nature. Larry Rasmussen, the present moderator of WCC's Unit III, concludes that the most significant feature of the following ecumenical discussions has been the reiterated emphasis on "sustainable society." He claims, rightly, that the international vocabulary received the phrase "the integrity of creation" from the World Council, and from the Council comes the frequent use of "sustainability" and "sustainable society," though not "sustainable development." "'Sustainability,' whether attached to 'development' or 'society,' has come to mean something very different in the WCC and other Non-governmental Organization circles from its prevailing notion in the UN, business, finance, and Northern nation-state government circles. It means, *not* global economic growth qualified by environmental sensitivity, but local and regional communities that are economically viable, socially equitable, and environmentally renewable."[13]

The theme of sustainability highlights that all the concerns, listed above, are interrelated, and that the interrelatedness is dynamic, not static. But as soon as the question about deployment of limited resources is asked, this very interrelatedness inevitably becomes a potential for conflict. Where to use which resources? The study of ecumenical social ethics shows that the concerns very often have clashed with conflict between the agents as a result. That goes a long way to explain the often tumultuous character of international ecumenical meetings.

The political approach to social ethics, as it has been developed within the ecumenical movement, is a project of Western modernity. As such it is a project of domesticating power and reducing the damages to life. But the shared assumptions of the good life on which this approach has been based are now dissolving into the particular agendas of different cultures, subcultures, and ethnic groups, and the conflicts may mount between the many agents with their widely differing scenarios of the needed change.

If one is content to understand the various institutions of the ecumenical movement as tools for domesticating political and economic power, one may expect the ecumenical network to help in organizing the conflicts by providing platforms for marginalized groups and peoples, so that they, too, may participate in the clash of cultures. But one may also expect the ecumenical institutions to become superfluous, because they have nothing or very little to contribute but what secular people already know themselves.

(2) "Costly Unity"

It is my assessment of the present state of the ecumenical movement that skepticism towards the inherited political logic of ecumenical organizations and a political approach to "doing the truth in charity" has at least set in. It is in that light that I read the most recent "ecclesiology-ethics" reports.[14] They attempt to regain a sense that being a Christian is to be a citizen of a different polis—a social narrative or community, set between memory and hope, in which we are formed into a different ethos and a different worldview by constantly being confronted with the story of the crucified and resurrected Christ.

Costly Unity, the first of these reports, claims that faith and discipleship are embodied in a communitarian way of life. This claim assumes a complex reality, where attention to what generates faith and discipleship cannot be separated from the community generated. By the story of the great things God has done that it tells, by the kind of community it becomes by attending to this and not to other stories, by the worship that it institutionalizes, by the way of reading the world that it encourages, and by the kind of questions of culture and politics that the story compels it to become involved in, the community fosters a distinct way of living, which, in turn, is linked to the community and its attention to the anamnesis of Christ.

The point is the configuration of attention to story, to community, and to a distinct way of living in and reading the world. Not first one element and then another element, but a "single, integral, way of life, seeing, hearing, thinking, doing."[15] It follows that formation becomes an ecumenical malformation if we attend exclusively to one or another element.

a) Malformation occurs, where Christian congregations understand themselves exclusively as the *objects* of the Word of God, transmitted in an inerrant text or in selected canonized traditions, and not also as *subjects* or communal practices that will live out the story in both church and world. Practices are morally formative. And malformation occurs, when, for example, the celebration of the Eucharist has no bearing on the dismantling of walls between races and no connection to the spiritual and bodily hungers of the world.[16] Malformation is the outcome, when positions on controversial moral questions like abortion, homosexuality, and biotechnologies are understood to drop ready-made from heaven as the non-negotiable Word of God. They come with a shared way of life—with ways of ordering biblical narrative and sacraments, with pathways of reflection, and with specific ways of exercising authority and attending to the issues of world and humanity. Moral positions are part and parcel of a community ethos. It is not "merely" isolated moral issues that are potentially divisive, but moral issues embedded in a community's understanding of ecclesial identity. An ecumenical discussion on a moral issue thus only makes sense within a wider dialogue: Is the position consistent with the specific configuration within which it is supposed to be grounded? and Does this specific way of attending to story, community, and world show the marks of forming attention to other configurations, or does it confuse God's story with its own absolutized story?[17]

b) Ecumenical malformation also occurs when the telling of the story becomes subordinated to living in a certain Christian culture and telling *its* story, whereby the call to catholicity is ignored. The Christian community becomes a tribal church. Focusing, primarily or merely, on the synthesis of a community's way of life—the tone and quality of its ethos, its operative main edition of the Christian story, and its dominant picture of the things of the world—undercuts the resurrection story's ability to break open and extend the possible ways of living as a Christian community.

c) Assuming ecumenical malformation as a result of attending too exclusively to the issues, and to world and humanity raises the question: What is meant by such an attention?

Christians often take over from elsewhere the way of reading world and history and then, in a second step, try to apply theological insights to this supposedly authoritative reading of reality. And by "elsewhere" I mean argued accounts of society and history as well as a local culture's basic assumptions of what reality is all about.

But attending to the story means acquiring a specific way of seeing world and history, whereby we learn not only to affirm the peace of Jesus Christ, but to read world and history in such a way that the assumptions (in philosophies and in realpolitik) of the primacy of violence are unmasked:

unless we grasp that the characteristic form of God's dealing with us is the formation of a community that manifests the possibility of human healing and justice, and directs the world to the praise of its maker, we shall not see why there is a Eucharistic community there at all.[18]

The "ecclesiology-ethics" divide will not be easy to overcome. Ecumenical history shows that approaches shaped *either* by ecclesiology *or* by ethics have failed. The most recent attempts to bridge the gap may also fail to convince, but they proceed at least along a more promising track. Only by attending to the configurations of story, community, and a story-patterned way of reading the world might we learn to avoid idolatry, sustain the disciplines of community, and learn to live as Christians, not in a concocted, but in this brutal world, as communities practiced in relations of peace. Without evidences that a different polis with a different ethos is possible, the story loses its power to heal and to hurt.

If I would use only one phrase for saying what the ecumenical movement is all about, I would suggest this: Nurturing the sense of a people. It is easily said. It sounds pious. But like orthodoxy, orthopraxis is a never ending task.

In a paper prepared for the WCC's ecclesiology-ethics debate, Lewis S. Mudge enumerates a good many of the ills of the contemporary world, and sums up: "So we find ourselves in a situation in which the problems call for an urgent and unified response while, at the same time, the divisions [between the churches] call for a careful and thorough healing."[19] Not first one thing (some abstract, global ethics put together by adding up the remnants of modernity's visions) and then something else (some global religious unity made instrumental for securing the earth's survival), but the fostering of an *oikoumene,* a "communion of particular, local embodiments of acted-out, shared, obedience to the gospel."[20] A communion of communions of every race, tribe, nation, and language, whose identity and whole way of life is formed most deeply not by race, tribe, nation, and language, but by the community-generating remembrance of cross and resurrection into which we are drawn by the Spirit. Only as markers or reminders of the Holy Spirit's resurrection-power to create community, solidarity, and reconciliation may we hope to contribute, on our own terms, i.e. on the Spirit's terms, to the mending of creation and the healing of nations while directing the world to the praise of its maker.

Such nurturing of a sense of a people is no easy calling. Like most human beings, most churches are multiple, if not divided, selves.

The "implicit axioms" (not necessarily, and not always articulated) which guide the ethos of an individual or a local congregation are often at some remove from church leaders' articulation of a community way of life. That has probably always been the case, but the "upstairs-downstairs" gap is presently very evident in most churches. A liberal environment and/or the market approach to religion, where consumer preferences are a determinative factor, may be blamed. But the "upstairs-downstairs" gap also cuts the other way. Persistent non-acceptance may reveal that denominational guidelines of faith and morals no longer are perceived as being embedded in and deriving meaning from a formation in holy things which the faithful, in prayer and confession, will acknowledge as the working of the Holy Spirit. Differing positions on women's ordination, on sex, and on the ascetic disciplines needed for being a sustainable community within the natural world provide some examples.

Gaining a sense of a people, a multifaceted community of trust and life-sustaining practices, will seem a "mission impossible" to both the prophets of inevitable culture wars and the trumpeters of a planetary apocalypse now. But it is what faith in God, the Holy Spirit, the Giver and gift of life, is all about. Commitment to such faith is not for the timid, the fainthearted, and the linesmen. It directs us to live in acceptance of a grace which does not leave our irrelations, destructiveness, and preferences for the familiar and the past unchanged and untransformed:

> It is in the occurrence of community, in the redemptive transformation of irrelation, that the breathing of God's Spirit, the movement of God's self-gift, is transcribed into the facts and possibilities of the world.[21]

The "anatomy" of both nature and social systems, including the churches, is porous to the Spirit, and that is gospel or "good news." The Spirit works in the details; it connects and enlivens. By the working of the Holy Spirit new configurations, new possibilities, and new reality come into being. Love and faithfulness come together, justice and peace embrace, community occurs. Among churches. Among peoples. Connections emerge. Among humankind and otherkind. Among social systems and natural systems:

> (When the Spirit from on high) will be poured upon *us*
> then shall the *wilderness* be *fertile land*
> and fertile land become forest.
> In the wilderness *justice* will come to live
> and *integrity* in the fertile land;
> integrity will bring *peace*,
> justice lasting *security*.
> *My people* will live in a peaceful home. . . . (Is. 32:15–18)

The only *oikoumene* that has any content in the midst of poisoned relationships and idolatrous worship of things and thought is an oikoumene or an "energy-field" of the Spirit's connecting and redemptive presence. What we can do, and by grace might do, is to recognize the resonances of the Spirit's community-generating politics in diverse communities of faith and fashion these resonances into a fabric of common life.[22] That task has no endings, and it does, thank God, not begin from the scratch of our deep divisions. It translates into "walking *in* the Spirit."

Notes

1. Cf. Konrad Raiser, *Report of the General Secretary,* WCC, Central Committee, Sept. 1996.

2. See *The Christian Century,* August 14, 1996.

3. Cf. Michael Root, "The Unity of the Church and the Reality of the Denominations," in *Modern Theology* 4 (1993), with references to a number of U.S. surveys.

4. Towards a Common Understanding and Vision of the World Council of Churches, A Working Draft for a Policy statement, Geneva, November 1996.

5. Cf. G. Lemopoulos, ed., *The Ecumenical Movement, the Churches and the World Council of Churches: An Orthodox Contribution to the Reflection Process on "The Common Understanding and Vision of the WCC"* (Geneva and Syndesmos, 1996). See Metropolitan John of Pergamon's contribution on 37ff.

6. Cf. "Final Document of the Chambésy Consultation," in *The Ecumenical Movement* (note 5), 12.

7. "First Official Report of RCC/WCC Joint Working Group," *Ecumenical Review* 2 (1996) 244. I am indebted to Thomas F. Stransky for the research on the beginnings of the phrase "the one ecumenical movement."

8. *The Decree on Ecumenism: Translation and Commentary* (New York, 1966).

9. This and similar expressions in the "Joint Working Group Second Report," *Ecumenical Review* 4 (1967), 461ff.

10. Cf. Heinrich Fries and Karl Rahner, *Einigung der Kirchen—reale Möglichkeit*, 3rd ed. (Freiburg, 1983).

11. A recent assessment in Konrad Raiser, "Ecumenical Discussion of Ethics and Ecclesiology," *Ecumenical Review* 1 (1996), 3ff.

12. I have used Peter Scherle's draft for the "History of Ecumenical Social Thought and Action" (Unit III, WCC, Geneva).

13. Larry L. Rasmussen, *Earth Community Earth Ethics* (Maryknoll, NY, 1997), 141–42.

14. *Costly Unity; Costly Commitment;* and *Costly Obedience* (Geneva 1993, 1995, and 1997).

15. Cf. *Costly Obedience: Toward an Ecumenical Communion of Moral Witnessing* (forthcoming). I quote from the final draft.

16. Cf. Larry L. Rasmussen, "Moral Community and Moral Formation," *Ecumenical Review* 2 (1995), 181ff.

17. Cf. "The Ecumenical Dialogue on Moral Issues: Potential Sources of Common Witness or of Divisions: A Study Document of the Joint Working Group," *Ecumenical Review* 2 (1996), 143ff.

18. Rowan Williams, "Imagining the Kingdom: Some Questions for Anglican Worship Today," in *The Identity of Anglican Worship*, ed. K. Stevenson et al. (London, 1991), 10.

19. Lewis S. Mudge, "Ecclesiology and Ethics in Current Ecumenical Debate," *Ecumenical Review* 1 (1996), 12, quoting William Henn in *Ecumenical Review* 2 (1995), 145. The phrase "the sense of a people" is the title of a book by Lewis S. Mudge: *The Sense of a People: Toward a Church for the Human Future* (Philadelphia, 1992).

20. *Costly Obedience*, quoted from the final draft.

21. Nicholas Lash, *Easter in Ordinary* (Notre Dame, Ind., 1998), 283.

22. Cf. *Costly Obedience*, which draws upon Michael Welker, *Gottes Geist: Theologie des Heiligen Geistes* (1992).

SIX

Three Morning
Biblical Meditations

Peter Coleman

∞

Our morning meditations are based on three psalms, 2, 22, and 145, with an introduction taken from Psalm 122: "Jerusalem is a city that is at unity in itself" (Ps. 122:3). You may be surprised that our basic texts are from the psalms—I can only say that when I began to think of a theme, this verse from Psalm 122 came to mind, and I have thought it worth pursuing, for three simple reasons: (1) our subject is unity; (2) we are in Jerusalem, and whatever our Confessional differences, we know that this holy city is highly significant for both Judaism and Christianity; and (3) the central role Jerusalem had in Israel's faith is for us transmuted into the symbol of our eschatological hope of Christ's final victory. "We look for the Holy City yet to come—the new Jerusalem coming down from Heaven, prepared as a bride adorned for her husband" (Rev. 21:2).

For many Christians, phrases from the psalms are among the most familiar parts of the Old Testament. That's because psalms (or parts of them) are included in almost every act of worship we attend, and so they lodge in our memory, as they always have in the Church's history.

From the beginning, Jewish converts to Christianity brought with them Israel's old poetry. Probably, the Apostles and Jesus himself would have known some of them by heart. Then, the early church found in the psalms prophecies and perceptions about the Messiah which linked the hopes of Old Israel with their experience of the life and work of Jesus. So the psalms became the most quoted Old Testament texts to be found in the New and were integrated into the developing forms of Christian worship.

At the Reformation, Calvin urged that they should continue to be used in a metric version so that "the Christians could sing the Scriptures"—as we still do, albeit in many different translations. The first Psalter in English was the work of Miles Coverdale, using the Vulgate and Luther's Bible as sources—thoroughly ecumenical! Coverdale's work was used in the Book of Common Prayer, still much valued in the Anglican communion. As old as Shakespeare, the language seems to remain more accessible to modern minds, but there is a risk that we understand less than we suppose we do of the meaning of the original.

What happens is this. By frequent recital and chanting over many years, we acquire, by a kind of osmosis, a welter of spiritual images which lodge in our hearts and minds as great truths about God. But this riot of images lodges in our minds without the kind of critical scrutiny that we would regard as commonplace for, say, the Gospels. Ignorant of the original *Sitz im Leben,* we attach our own, not realizing that we may have missed the original point. Of course, we do sometimes spot the inconsistencies between the theology of the psalms and Christian beliefs, as when our consciences grate at the cursing passages. No harm, we may say; poetry is not to be tested for doctrinal orthodoxy, but we should also remember Leonard Hodgson's helpful dictum: "What must the truth have been, and be, if people who thought like that wrote it down like this." Taking that advice, what shall we make of Psalm 122?

Psalm 122 (Coverdale)

1 I was glad when they said unto me: We will go into the house of the Lord.
2 Our feet shall stand in thy gates: O Jerusalem.
3 Jerusalem is built as a city: that is at unity in itself.

4 For thither the tribes go up, even the tribes of the Lord: to
testify unto Israel, to give thanks unto the name of the Lord.
5 For there is the seat of judgement: even the seat of the house
of David.
6 O pray for the peace of Jerusalem: they shall prosper that love
thee.
7 Peace be within thy walls: and plenteousness within thy
palaces.
8 For my brethren and companions' sakes: I will seek to do
thee good.

The opening words of this psalm have become for the English a
kind of substitute national anthem, somewhat akin to the American
custom of playing "Hail to the Chief" whenever the president arrives.
Herbert Parry wrote a splendid tune to this psalm for our present
queen's coronation in 1953, and it's the obvious choice for cathedral
choirs on royal occasions. But it was not originally a psalm associated
with the king's enthronement in Jerusalem; it was composed as a personal meditation.

I see a thoughtful pilgrim trying to sum up in a few words his impression of a first visit to Jerusalem in the days of the monarchy. He
was glad he was asked to go. He came perhaps from one of the Judean
tribes settled on the coastal plain, and climbing the hill, he caught his
first sight of the Temple—all the domestic buildings were then kept
out of the way on the southern slope. The shrine, the king's palace,
and the surrounding wall dominated, and he could see the unity of the
design.

Actually, the Hebrew says literally, "Jerusalem was compact," and
our poet turns that into a spiritual vision. We Jews have a special
covenant with Jahweh. We are not just scattered tribes, we are one
people, our religion and our political leadership are bound together in
one theocracy. The topography of the Holy City is used as a model of
the unity God wills for his people. It is no longer sufficient to identify
oneself as of the tribe of Benjamin; seeing Jerusalem, our pilgrim's
vision is stretched, enhanced; he belongs to God's larger family.

This singular vision became, as we know, a favorite song for subsequent visitors to Jerusalem. They sung it at the bottom of the steps,

before ascending to the Temple Mount. "I was glad when they said unto me, we will go up to the House of the Lord." But then as now, Jerusalem, the city of unity, was divided against itself, a place of tension and weeping, rather than joy. When Christ saw it, he wept.

So to the second psalm for this morning, very different in its imagery, severe rather than affirming. If the pilgrim meditation of Psalm 122 cheers us in a rather romantic way, Psalm 2 brings us back to earthly reality with a bump.

Psalm 2 (Coverdale)

1 Why do the heathen so furiously rage together: and why do the people imagine a vain thing?
2 The kings of the earth stand up, and the rulers take counsel together: against the Lord, and against his Anointed.
3 Let us break their bonds asunder: and cast away their cords from us.
4 He that dwelleth in heaven shall laugh them to scorn: the Lord shall have them in derision.
5 Then shall he speak unto them in his wrath: and vex them in his sore displeasure.
6 Yet have I set my King: upon my holy hill of Sion.
7 I will preach the law, whereof the Lord hath said unto me: Thou art my Son, this day have I begotten thee.
8 Desire of me, and I shall give thee the heathen for thine inheritance: and the utmost parts of the earth for thy possession.
9 Thou shalt bruise them with a rod of iron: and break them in pieces like a potter's vessel.
10 Be wise now therefore, O ye kings: be learned, ye that are judges of the earth.
11 Serve the Lord in fear: and rejoice unto him with reverence.
12 Kiss the Son, lest he be angry, and so ye perish from the right; if his wrath be kindled, (yea, but a little,) blessed are all they that put their trust in him.

This is an enthronement psalm, it was used both at the accession of Israel's kings, and at the annual Festival service at the Temple, commemorating the event.

It begins with a question: "Why do the heathen so furiously rage together, and why do the rulers of the earth imagine a vain thing?" We can put that in modern English as "Why do the nations rage, and the people plot in vain?" This text is of course marvelously used in Handel's Messiah, and clearly the theme is defiance.

In the ancient world of the Middle East, changing the king was a dangerous event causing great turbulence. Most people of that world belonged to conquered vassal states, owing unwilling obedience to a foreign and often distant ruler. When he died, hopes of independence soared. Why should we remain victims? Let us regain our sovereignty. While the new ruler is busy sorting out his immediate problems at home, let us claim our proper freedom. But, says this psalm, they have forgotten who Israel's real king is. Sovereignty belongs to Jahweh, and he laughs at the pretensions of all the nations. Kings rule by his appointment or concession, even the alien Cyrus, "rod of God's anger," as Isaiah has it. Attempts to defy God are useless.

When David is crowned, he is adopted as God's son, but this is not understood in Israel as total divinization, in the pattern of Egypt and other neighbors. Note the careful wording—"This day have I begotten thee." Yes, thou art my adopted son, but only while you represent me correctly and while you rightly expound my will to the people. If you do not, you are deposed. Israel's kings are not divinized, they rule under holy obedience only.

Now consider verse 10. Be wise therefore you vassal kings, lest you be broken like a potter's vessel. The uncomfortable fact you have to face is that Jahweh, the true ruler of Jerusalem, presents you with an unavoidable choice: Serve me or perish! Like it or not, this psalm presents us with the stark totalitarian religious challenge—obey God or be damned! God meets human defiance with his own resolution.

Moderns do not find this intransigence comfortable. In other psalms, while this rigor in proclaiming the ultimate sovereignty of God is not abandoned, it is balanced in vastly reassuring ways. If the defiant God of Jerusalem depicted in Psalm 2 seems too fierce and frightening to be accepted, then we shall find in other psalms hints and glimpses of the healing Gospel.

Psalm 22 (Coverdale)

1 My God, my God, look upon me; why hast thou forsaken me: and art so far from my health, and from the words of my complaint?

2 O my God, I cry in the day-time, but thou hearest not: and in the night-season also I take no rest.

3 And thou continuest holy: O thou worship of Israel.

4 And our fathers hoped in thee: they trusted in thee, and thou didst deliver them.

5 They called upon thee, and were helpen: they put their trust in thee, and were not confounded.

6 But as for me, I am a worm, and no man: a very scorn of men, and the outcast of the people.

7 All they that see me laugh me to scorn: they shoot out their lips, and shake their heads, saying,

8 He trusted in God, that he would deliver him: let him deliver him, if he will have him.

9 But thou art he that took me out of my mother's womb: thou wast my hope, when I hanged upon my mother's breasts.

10 I have been left unto thee ever since I was born: thou art my God even from my mother's womb.

11 O go not from me, for trouble is hard at hand: and there is none to help me.

12 Many oxen are come about me: fat bulls of Basan close me in on every side.

13 They gape upon me with their mouths: as it were a ramping and roaring lion.

14 I am poured out like water, and all my bones are out of joint: my heart also in the midst of my body is even like melting wax.

15 My strength is dried up like a potsherd, and my tongue cleaveth to my gums: and thou shalt bring me into the dust of death.

16 For many dogs come about me: and the council of the wicked layest siege against me.

17 They pierced my hands and my feet; I may tell all my bones: they stand staring and looking upon me.

18 They part my garments among them: they cast lots upon my vesture.

19 But be not thou far from me, O Lord: thou art my succour, haste thee to help me.

20 Deliver my soul from the sword; my darling from the power of the dog.

21 Save me from the lion's mouth: thou hast heard me also from among the horns of the unicorns.

22 I will declare thy name unto my brethren: in the midst of the congregation will I praise thee.

23 O praise the Lord, ye that fear him: magnify him, all ye of the seed of Jacob, and fear him, all ye seed of Israel;

24 For he hath not despised, nor abhorred, the low estate of the poor: he hath not hid his face from him, but when he called unto him he heard him.

25 My praise is of thee in the great congregation: my vows will I perform in the sight of them that fear him.

26 The poor shall eat, and be satisfied: they that seek after the Lord shall praise him; your heart shall live for ever.

27 All the ends of the word shall remember themselves, and be turned unto the Lord: and all the kindreds of the nations shall worship before him.

28 For the kingdom is the Lord's: and he is the Governor among the people.

29 All such as be fat upon earth: have eaten, and worshipped.

30 All they that go down into the dust shall kneel before him: and no man hath quickened his own soul.

31 My seed shall serve him: they shall be counted unto the Lord for a generation.

32 They shall come, and the heavens shall declare his
   righteousness: unto a people that shall be born, whom
   the Lord hath made.

The opening verse of this psalm is deeply lodged in the awareness
of Christian people because of its link with Our Lord's cry from the
cross. But before we consider that, we can allow this psalm its own
original character—it is an individual lamentation, a profound study
of the struggle between faith and doubt, the personal story of someone
in extreme pain and facing death.

We do not know, of course, exactly what predicament surrounds
the author. It may have been a severe and painful illness which was apparently life-threatening. Those around him expect him to die, and
he has reached the same conclusion about himself. Hope of recovery
is slipping away, and so he is thrust acutely into the dilemma that all
believers know. Even now, would it not be possible for God to inter-
vene? This is the standard struggle of the soul in extremis. It seems my
time has come. I must go to Sheol and join my ancestors in that grey
sombre world from which no visitor returns.

But the misery depicted here may not be just terminal disease. It
could be the cry of a prisoner facing execution. We need not go so far
as to guess that this is Daniel, crying from his cell by the lion's den as
he hears their hungry growling of anticipation. We know enough of
the political situation of tiny Israel amidst powerful warring nations to
expect that many Jews would be captured, imprisoned, and killed.
There are hints that the author is a captive, taken away from his home.

But as you can see, there are some verses here which do not fit the
situation of a prisoner of war. Verses 6–8 describe a scene of public
mockery, not just of a captive. He is scorned as an outcast, an *Unter-
mensch,* not because of his nationality, but apparently because of his
beliefs. He trusts and hopes his God will deliver him from his predicament. What a vain hope. How ridiculous that he refuses to face facts.

I have recently been reading an account by a former bishop of the
churches' life in Eastern Germany during the period of communist
rule. The hardest task, he found, was to keep faith under the constant
assault of secular mockery. Christians were dismissed as clinging to re-
dundant beliefs, and gradually the support of nominal and conven-

tional Christians ebbed away. Doubt sapped their commitment, they could not remain standing by the cross. But we must not move too quickly to Golgotha and the passion of Christ.

The problem of pain, the inevitability of death is a familiar theme of the psalms, and Judaism had no easy answer, any more than Christianity does. In principle, to the religious mind, it always seems an outrage that a good person cannot escape suffering and death. But for the Fall, as the ancients say, when our time comes, we could march comfortably out of this life straight through the gates of heaven! And whenever a person of faith struggles with death, he will be met by fatalism. Watching good people die is a standard invitation to atheism. As an old soldier once put it to me, "Padre, I have seen too many good people die to have any faith left myself." The early verses of this psalm fully reflect that great theological dilemma. Hope and trust ought to lead to deliverance, so he cries out "thou wast my hope when I still hanged on my mother's breast." Why have I come to this?

But as you can see the mood of the poem, and the thrust of its argument changes dramatically at verse 19, and from verse 22 we are in a mood of escape and recovery. Our captive is going back to his people. "I will declare thy name among the congregation"—so our prisoner is back in Israel—and verse 23 begins his hymn of praise, a kind of Old Testament *Te Deum*.

The Early Church frequently used selected psalms to explore and explain the work of Christ, and this is of course the best known example. Some critics of the passion narrative in Mark and Matthew think the quotations from this psalm were put into the mouth of the dying Jesus by the synoptic authors as thoroughly appropriate glosses—thus verse 18, "they parted my garments," etc.

More cautious scholars reckon Jesus would have known this psalm and found in it words to express his inner agony. Have you noticed that dying people often whisper the "Our Father" to ease their anxiety? So Jesus may well have muttered the whole psalm to himself as the moment of testing came upon him. If he did, he would have found comfort in the later verses, as our prisoner did. In other words, Christ does not die in despair, but looking forward in faith. That corresponds to the fourth Gospel's account, which ends on a more confident note. The final cry is *Tetelesti*: it is accomplished.

I had an interesting confirmation of the value of reading Psalm 22 as a guide to the passion this recently passed Good Friday. In our Anglican tradition, many churches have a special devotional service that day—three hours from midday, or one hour until 3 P.M., the traditional time of Christ's death. This year, I suggested that after 3 P.M., before leaving church, the members of the congregation might like to read through the whole of Psalm 22 slowly, to see how well it summed up for them the devotional journey they had been making. It would help them to understand the journey of the passion and look forward in quiet confidence to Easter Eve and the glory of the resurrection. After the service one lady remained in her pew, obviously reading intently. She told me later that she was a divinity teacher, had spent twenty years teaching the atonement to children from the passion narrative and never before realized how Psalm 22 was used in it. So, like Christ, we value this psalm as a strong resource at desperate moments, it carries us from despair to affirmation.

Psalm 145 (Coverdale)

1 I will magnify thee, O my God, My King: and I will praise thy name for ever and ever.

2 Every day will I give thanks unto thee: and praise thy name for ever and ever.

3 Great is the Lord, and marvellous worthy to be praised: there is no end of his greatness.

4 One generation shall praise thy works unto another: and declare thy power.

5 As for me, I will be talking of thy worship: thy glory, thy praise, and wondrous works;

6 So that men shall speak of the might of thy marvellous acts: and I will also tell of thy greatness.

7 The memorial of thine abundant kindness shall be shewed: and men shall sing of thy righteousness.

8 The Lord is gracious, and merciful: long-suffering, and of great goodness.

9 The Lord is loving unto every man: and his mercy is over all his works.

10 All thy works praise thee, O Lord: and thy saints give thanks unto thee.

11 They shew the glory of thy kingdom: and talk of thy power;

12 That thy power, thy glory, and mightiness of thy kingdom: might be known unto men.

13 Thy kingdom is an everlasting kingdom: and thy dominion endureth throughout all ages.

14 The Lord upholdeth all such as fall: and lifteth up all those that are down.

15 The eyes of all wait upon thee, O Lord: and thou givest them their meat in due season.

16 Thou openest thine hand: and fillest all things living with plenteousness.

17 The Lord is righteous in all his ways: and holy in all his works.

18 The Lord is nigh unto all them that call upon him: yea, all such as call upon him faithfully.

19 He will fulfil the desire of them that fear him: he also will hear their cry, and will help them.

20 The Lord preserveth all them that love him: but scattereth abroad all the ungodly.

21 My mouth shall speak the praise of the Lord: and let all flesh give thanks unto his holy name for ever and ever.

We are working through these selected psalms in a simple threefold plan. First, we recall what these psalms meant for God's people, Israel. Second, we note how these timeless perceptions of truth about God and his ways were adopted into early Christian worship, and then we see how they work for us today. We realize that the continual use of psalms in our prayer lodges in our minds a riot of images, by a process which I call spiritual osmosis. We test that process by asking "What must the truth have been, and be, if people who thought like that wrote it down like this?"

Following this plan, we come now to Psalm 145, which is a community hymn of praise, and you will note that this cheerful song lacks the drama of our previous studies. Psalm 122 spoke of the eschatological unity of Jerusalem, and with Psalm 2, in contrast, we confronted God's mocking defiance of all human attempts to preserve their own autonomy.

We studied Psalm 22, so familiar to us from the passion narratives, setting out God's reassuring commitment to face suffering and rejection with his people. If Jerusalem is a place where God defies the world, it is also the place where he redeems it. Psalm 145 extends that vision of redemption to include all nature and all humankind. It follows logically the claim of Psalm 22 that if God laughs at human pretension, he also gathers all things and all people into his providence and the offer of salvation.

This psalm is a splendid example of God's people singing scriptural truth, as Calvin put it; and in fact, the best loved Reformation hymn, "*Lobe den Herren*," is Herrenschmidt's rendering of this psalm. A similar version, probably better known to us, comes from Neander. And of course in Judaism, this psalm is included in daily prayer. Its original provenance is thought to be the Autumn Feast of the Covenant.

Verses 1–6 spread out the proclamation—Great is God, known in his name which declares his marvelous acts. The names we give to people are very important. If we are not our names, who are we? We have no identity and no value. Thus Saint Paul, on the Areopagus before the Altar to the Unknown God announces, "This God whom you ignorantly worship we declare unto you." Some years ago, there was a very cruel cartoon in the magazine *Punch*. It depicted a farewell presentation to an old, long-serving employee. The fat managing director begins his speech: "We are gathered here to thank one of our company's most valued servants . . . dear old what's his name."

One of the snags of growing older, I find, is not just the difficulty of forgetting the names of people I know well, but the greater difficulty of reassuring them that I do know who they are, and my misnaming them is not a sign that I have lost my regard for them. So, in this psalm, we praise God in his name, because that is his character and his importance. It is *anamnesis,* the act of recalling, which makes the past event real for the present.

Establishing first the name of the Lord, the mighty acts follow, chiefly creation and providence. These days, for most Christians, I suppose, the science versus faith debate is virtually over. We can hold together comfortably the riot of images provided by Scripture and the sciences. The fascinating, if constantly changing, pictures of the universe astronomers send us from their space stations and the equally vivid cosmology of Genesis, with which this psalm and many others beguile us, mingle in our minds. Taken together, this riot of images enlarges our grasp of God's creative magic. If you have time and security permits, go and sit in the shepherd's field on the other side of Bethlehem as the stars begin to loom out of the dusk. Then say to yourself, "Thou spreadest out the heavens like a curtain," and there glows that satellite by which God lets us send our faxes home.

These days, I find Christians enjoy learning about the cosmology of the Bible. God made a flat earth and above it a hemisphere like an upturned pudding basin. He made it of one-way, see-through glass, so that he could watch us clearly, but we could only see him dimly. Of course, they think its not really like that, and yet of course it is exactly like that—what Ian Ramsey used to call a disclosure situation of complementary truths. Multi-model reality is good news. It makes Scripture live, and we escape from the false dilemma of having to choose between biblical fundamentalism and taking the photos that the astronauts send back from their space station as all there is to be said. So God up there, God out there, God down here, God in the midst of things. Once we learn to live with all this riot of images, we are preserved from the fear that perhaps he is nowhere at all.

I daresay that the Israeli patriarchs, sitting around their campfire with the stars glinting above them, had their own arguments about what was really out there, but for the author of Psalm 145, the important thing was to proclaim God's power and God's acts. How he did it all was a question that humans should not pretend to understand in detail. Models were enough—as any modern scientist would say of his own explanations.

From verse 8 onwards, a new theme emerges—this mighty ruler is gracious, abounding in loving kindness. Modern translators have searched for the best equivalent to *Hesed*. The RSV has "steadfast love." The old debate about agape, philia, and eros has dropped out of view these days. As we understand better the steadfastness of God to his covenant, there is no change in his attitude, whatever the disappointment or provocation. He lifts up all those who are down.

Now we come to two verses which have been used most widely as an introduction to grace before meats, as it once was called: "The eyes of all things look up and put their trust in Thee O Lord, Thou openest Thy hand and fillest all things."

This Coverdale language has a special association for me. In early life I trained as a barrister, and that required me to attend a series of formal dinners at my Inn of Court. Before we sat down at the long tables in this medieval Middle Temple hall, the Inn's treasurer, in fact a senior judge, would intone these verses, followed by "Good Lord, bless this food to our use and ourselves to your service." I now know that it is not only lawyers who use this grace, it is common among all kinds of professional and academic societies.

Over the years, I have somewhat lost my simple attitude to it. Grace before meats, but not before fish, I was told; but that won't do for Fridays, nor does it seem likely Jesus made this distinction after the great draught of fishes. As we trudge around the food supermarkets, worrying about ecology and the food chain, a gentle musing on these verses seems appropriate.

Finally, note verse 7: "The memorial of thy abundant kindness shall be shown." The RSV has "they shall pour forth the fame of thy abundant goodness." More accurate but what a pity. I used to think this was an ideal Old Testament text to pre-figure the Eucharist, for surely this is where we begin our explanation of the Lord's Supper. It is the chief memorial of thy abundant kindness.

In the end, the *Hesed,* the loving steadfastness of God is not only to Israel but to all nature and all men. When he has to, God defies human arrogance, but he offers to carry human suffering himself. When the roundness of his nature and his name is discerned, he is the Creator and Sustainer of all things, watching over all with steadfast love.

There is a famous broadcasting rabbi on a Monday morning BBC program, Rabbi Lionel Blue. As I finished drafting these meditations I heard him say this:

Religion goes through the same developments as a baby. It begins by loving itself, then it loves its mother. Then it has to love its family. Finally it has, God willing, to make the great leap of loving other people. Sadly, some religious people fail to make this leap and get diverted into loving real estate.

This is where we came in. I was glad when they said unto me, let us go to the House of the Lord. The ecumenical challenge is to move on from there to love all the tribes of Israel, new and old.

SEVEN

The Rift That Binds:
Hermeneutical Approaches to the
Jewish-Christian Relationship

Michael A. Signer

∞

During the past fifty years, particularly since the promulgation of *Nostra Aetate* in 1965, the relationship between Jews and Christians has been moving slowly and inexorably from "disputation" to "dialogue," from confrontation to community. The difficulty of establishing trust between our communities grows out of a painful theological tradition which has often led to violence. We continue to formulate statements about each other as a monolithic entity—as simply "Christians" or "Jews" without taking into full account the nuanced differences of theology and practice which constitute those who call themselves Christians or Jews. It has been the result of continuous striving and enormous good will during the past half-century that we can assemble at Tantur in Jerusalem and speak with each other—heeding the words of the Psalmist, "Behold how good and how pleasant it is for brothers to dwell together in unity" (Ps. 133:1).

It may even seem incongruous to present a paper on Judaism as part of a conference on "ecumenism." Ecumenism and interreligious dialogue ought to constitute two entirely independent conversations. From their own perspective, members of the contemporary Jewish community do not understand themselves as participants in the Christian "household." Most sympathetic Christians do not comprehend them as belonging to their *ecclesia* or even to the most broadly understood definition of the "body of Christ." However, when we consider the etymology of the word *oekoumene* which provides the basis for our English word "ecumenical," we recognize that it means "household." At that level the Jewish people would join with Christians in a self-consciousness of participation in the household of those who call upon the God of Israel.

The location of the conference here at Tantur in *Erez Yisrael* or "on the way to Bethlehem" also serves as a sign that the "household of Israel" has new meaning for our relationship as Christians and Jews. For the first time in nearly two thousand years, Jews in the Land and throughout the world have our own "household," our state, and we are engaged in the painful process of learning the pleasures and the perils of responsible proprietorship.

Aside from the unique living dialogue in the land of Israel, we Jews are part of the extended household of Christians because, as Martin Buber nicely said, we share with you a book and a hope. The book of Scripture and the hope for an era of peace and justice point toward the same end, which our communities in the world reach by very different paths of worship and reflection. We have learned about our mutual beginnings and ends as a result of very intense and painful explorations during these past decades of our new relationship.

As Jewish communities, we have discovered during the last thirty years that ecumenism and interreligious relations have a certain homology within the structure of the Catholic Church. To a certain extent they provide the appropriate directions for the ebb and flow of our conversations. Jewish concerns with the Catholic Church are addressed to the Pontifical Commission for Relationship with the Jews, which constitutes part of the Pontifical Council for Christian Unity. In the American Catholic context, it is most often the ecumenical officer to whom the duty of engaging in discussions with the Jews is entrusted. Therefore, we might now claim that it is entirely fitting for a paper on Judaism to be part of a significant discourse about the future of intra-Christian relations. It points to a paradox that from some perspectives the unity we seek may be a unity within diversity.

The discordance of unity within diversity animates this essay. A division may provide the ground for engagement and encounter between Jews and Christians. It is my conviction that the grace of contemporary theological reflection is that it interrupts our commonplace ways of thought and calls upon us to engage the teachings of our traditions within the broadest horizons possible. We become interpreters of interpretation bringing the past into the present and the present to the past. In recognizing our ability to collapse and expand temporality, we find the courage or indeed audacity to urge or exhort our fellow humans to make the changes necessary for the future which is outlined but not fulfilled.

During the course of this paper I hope to draw upon divergent sources for interpretation: my own experiences of engagement with Christian-Jewish dialogue, both in American and European contexts; as well as the textual sources of our Jewish and Christian exegetical traditions. It is my hope that this paper will be a meditation on both tradition and experience, which will ultimately lead to a theoretical framework for future discussions of the Jewish-Christian relationship and its goal.

Experience, the reality of face to face conversation, has become an important teacher in this newly discovered relationship between Christians and Jews. In many ways our experience of each other in sincere and open discussion has far outstripped our theory for explicating the foundations and future directions of the dialogue. Oral conversations and collaborative projects have multiplied much faster than the number of reflective essays on the theological or philosophical dimensions of those conversations and actions.[1] Jewish-Christian discussions provide a very important paradigm for the appropriate relationship of theory and praxis: at their best they exist in dialectical relationship with each other—correcting and nurturing greater movement.[2] Abraham Joshua Heschel indicated this preeminence of experience in his essay "No Religion Is an Island," when he said, "First and foremost, we meet as human beings who have much in common: a heart, a face, a voice, the presence of a soul, fears, hope, the ability to trust, a capacity for compassion and understanding, the kinship of being human, a solidarity of being."[3] Our starting point for Jewish-Christian dialogue is the common experience of our humanity—and in the discovery of our humanity—our "being for the Other" as Emmanuel Levinas has phrased it so felicitously—and then we may move toward an examination of the rich sources within our theological traditions and bring new insights forth from them.[4]

The paper will be divided into three parts: an introduction which focuses on the power of the "image" to stimulate discussion about the dimensions of Jewish-Christian relations, then we will explore two "images" developed nineteen hundred years apart. The first image comes from St. Paul's Epistle to the Romans, chapter 11, of the "olive tree." The second image, the "star and the rays," derives from *The Star of Redemption* composed by the German-Jewish theologian Franz Rosenzweig (1886–1929). After the "olive tree" and the "star" we will turn to a third image of the "rift" or "seam" as a potential corrective for reframing future discussions of our relationship. At the conclusion of the paper, we will introduce a new direction for Christian-Jewish dialogue, the study of our exegetical traditions on the Hebrew Bible. We hope that the example of the Jacob and Esau narrative will provide new fecundity in our future dialogue.

Two personal experiences illuminate the beginning of our way in dialogue. In my first semester at the University of Notre Dame, I gave an undergraduate seminar on the Hebrew Chronicles of the First Crusade. One of my students who was in the process of discerning a vocation for the priesthood wrote a final examination which placed the blame for the massacres of the Rhenish Jewish community squarely on the shoulders of the Jews who were as he put it "exploiting the poor Christians with their usury." Needless to say, my comments on his final examination went far beyond correcting his serious misinterpretations of the Hebrew Chronicles and the materials from lectures and readings. I indicated that he might want to consider what it means to "blame the victim" and how far he might be from achieving empathy with those who suffered. These qualities might be very significant to his future as a priest. He never directly responded to my remarks about his paper. However I recently received a communication from him which illustrates the power of honest dialogue and response.

> I took your course in my senior year. To refresh your memory, I
> had that 'misunderstanding' in my final paper—apparently I came

across as placing some inappropriate blame in reference to the crusade chronicle.

I was reading a brief article about John Paul II reminding Christians to look to Hebrew Scriptures to understand their own faith and that tripped my memory of that paper.

I'm now a Maronite priest and I'm about to go to Pittsburgh as an assistant pastor. . . . I've been at Catholic University in Washington, D.C., and joined the Army Reserves as a chaplain candidate. I just wanted to let you know that your reaction to that paper has always stayed with me. In the army I've been dealing with a lot of issues of religious tolerance. Although I regret the misunderstanding occurred I'm grateful to have had the experience. I just wanted to let you know that your teaching has influenced my ministry as a priest in both the civilian and military spheres.

The second story also derives from teaching, but in a very different time and place. Two years ago I lectured in five institutes of Catholic higher learning in Poland: Warsaw, Lublin, Wroclaw, Poznan, and Krakow. For the most part I was elated by the reactions of young Polish students of theology. They were all enthusiastic and eager to learn more about Judaism. Many of them explicitly stated that they wanted to change the terrible traditions of anti-Semitism which had been part of the Polish Church.

However, one of the most valuable experiences for me occurred in Wroclaw during a lecture for candidates who would teach religion in high schools. At the conclusion of a lecture on Jewish liturgy, one student stood up and said, "I have heard nothing about Jesus Christ in your lecture this afternoon. Where is the dialogue? If there is no Jesus Christ there is no dialogue for the Christian." His colleagues gasped and there was palpable tension in the room. At the time I remember I was quite shocked by his strong reaction, so I spoke very clearly and with great passion. My response was that Christ was as Saint Paul had put it a *scandalum,* a stumbling block, between Christians and Jews. However, a dialogue takes place not where there is agreement for that would be a soliloquy or at best a monologue. True dialogue takes place when people who disagree discuss both similarity and difference. Perhaps Franz Rosenzweig, to whom we shall return later in this paper, put it best when he wrote about the "community and non-community" that Christians and Jews have shared. Dialogue may have more to do with being challenged than with being affirmed. Ultimately, we may find that our greatest moments of affirmation in dialogue with each other come out of the painful challenges of realizing the differences which are irreconcilable—and the strong bond which joins us despite our differences.

These personal stories indicate the possibility for dialogue as the grounds for transforming our understanding of each other. These perceptions or misperceptions are often the product of reflection or meditation on passages from Scripture or the literature of our traditions. The language of Scripture is rich in imagery of the natural world. Moments of revelation are charged with lightning and thunder. Passionate diatribes are delivered about the people of Israel as a vineyard. Later generations of students retain the image without evoking its context. The images themselves are capable of arousing piety or devotion.

The notion of image or icon has been productive for the religious traditions of Judaism and Christianity in the modern era as well. Reflection on images whether they are verbal or visual produce new insight and allow a significant retrieval of the past. Walter Benjamin, a Jewish thinker of Weimar Germany, described the relationship of image to temporality as follows.

> An image is that in which the Then and the Now come into a constellation like a flash of lightning. In other words: image is dialectics at a standstill. For while the relation of the present to the past is a purely temporal, continuous one, the relation to the Then and the Now is dialectical—not development, but image leaping forth.[5]

This rhapsodic description captures the capacity of image to collapse temporality and move both the intellect and the heart. An image provides the thinker or theologian with an occasion to capture present and past simultaneously for the purpose of breaking the thrall of rootlessness. In reflecting upon images, we can reestablish our grounding in tradition. By unlocking the power of the image we are able to move from present to past or from past to present—or, in a moment, to behold the future.

One of the most fecund images for theologians and thinkers of the Jewish-Christian relationship is to be found in Saint Paul's letter to the Romans 9–11. In 11:17, he concludes his long meditation on the relationship between his brethren in the house of Israel who have not believed in Jesus as the Christ by proposing the most striking image of the olive tree.

> If the root of the tree is consecrated, so are its branches. If some of the branches have been lopped off, you, though a branch from a wild olive tree, have been grafted into their place and have come to share in the rich sap of the olive root. Do not boast over those branches. If you do, remember this: you do not support the root; the root supports you.[6]

St. Paul employed the figure of an olive tree. It would have been familiar to those who read the Hebrew Bible as an apt representation of the people Israel. In the Hebrew Scripture, Jeremiah 11:16, we read, "The Lord called you [Israel] a green olive tree, fair in appearance which will be called to judgment." In this passage, the olive tree appears as a figure of Israel receiving prophetic rebuke. However, in Hosea 14:1–6, God promises to heal Israel's apostasy and love them because His anger is turned away from them. God will be as dew to Israel so that they will blossom and be as fair as the olive tree. The image of the olive tree could serve either as a positive or negative figure for Israel—depending upon their loyalty to the divine covenant.

In Romans, Paul depicts Israel as an olive tree consecrated to God at its core and root. They are beloved of God because of the divine faithfulness to the covenant with the ancestors (9:1–5). The gentiles or peoples from the pagan world draw upon the consecration of the tree itself from that very covenant. What is new for them is their grafting into the root as "wild olive branches" because they have believed in Christ.

Once Paul has proposed the figure of the olive tree, he turns it into a prophetic exhortation to those who have entered the Church in the new way. They are not to display arrogance or pride because the Jews who did not believe have been cut off the tree. God is righteous displaying "kindness" and "severity" depending upon loyalty. The Jews, if they come to believe, will not be forever cut off, or as J. Fitzmyer put it, "they are not cast off into a rubbish heap" (v. 23).[7] God is able to graft them in again. "For if you [the Gentiles] were cut from what is by nature a wild olive tree and grafted contrary to nature into a cultivated one, how much more will they who belong to it by nature be grafted back into their own olive tree" (v. 24).

The dialectical nature of God's free choice to bring the Gentiles into the covenant of "severity" and "mercy" and to hold them responsible for their actions is apparent in this passage. Paul indicates that the natural order is for Israel to enjoy the sacred covenant with God like the naturally growing olive tree. Israel's rejection of Christ, in contradiction to the 'natural order' has, therefore, led to the opportunity for the Gentiles to come to God. The contrast between "nature" and the grafting as an act of God's grace is evident from the argument that Israel's rejection is "a partial blindness" which will exist only until the fullness of the Gentiles shall have come in (v. 25). This act of grafting in the Gentiles contrary to nature and the restoration of the Jews is, in Paul's eyes, a *mysterium*, an act hidden in God to be revealed for the instruction of all.

The power of Paul's Epistle to the Romans is at the foundation of the conciliar document *Nostra Aetate* whose first phrase resonates with its ideas: *Mysterium Ecclesiae perscrutans, Sacra haec Synodus meminit vinculi quo populus Novi Testamenti cum stirpe Abrahae spiritualiter coniunctus est.*

We begin with the contemplation of the Mysterium of verse 25. Perhaps most significant is the idea of *coniunctus*—the Church is joined to the root of Abraham [*stirpe*]. The Fathers of the Council signaled that they were engaging in a new theological reflection on the relationship with Judaism. The issue of a theology of Judaism begins *inside* the boundaries of the Church itself. The Second Vatican Council's statement about Judaism was not a "public relations" gesture to assuage contemporary culture, but profoundly to be sought within Christian theology itself.

Romans 9–11 appears repeatedly in the teachings of Pope John Paul II who has insisted on the bond that exists between the Church as the people of the New Covenant and their unbreakable bond with the Old Covenant—and ultimately with the Jewish people.[8] Krister Stendahl and Paul van Buren have provided theologies of the Jewish-Christian relationship which allows for a very positive place for the Jewish people in God's salvation history and that put this relationship at the center of Christian theological reflection.[9]

Yet, with all the recent positive dimensions presented by St. Paul in Romans 11, it is significant to recall that in the early centuries of the interpretation there was no concept of post-incarnational salvation for the Jewish people at all.[10] With the death and resurrection of Jesus Christ only those who followed and believed participated in divine salvation. Paul's image of *excaecatio* (blindness) of the Jews became a literary maxim which generated the medieval three-dimensional representation of synagoga with her eyes veiled—blinded to the truth of Christ—while the triumphant *ecclesia* gazed forward with her eyes clearly revealed.[11] Paul's olive tree image does not immediately yield a positive estimation of post-incarnational Israel. Abraham's descendant Isaac, whom Paul taught was the type of Christ both in Galatians and Romans, allows for a theological framework which places no value on the continuity of the Jewish people as God's covenanted people through time. God awaits Israel to turn to Christ at the eschaton for the ultimate regrafting of the natural olive branches into their root. Only then is the Jewish people fully Israel.

Despite the negative assessments of Israel in Paul's figure of the olive tree, Jews have also, albeit often unconsciously, adopted the image of the tree to describe their relationship with Christians. They understand themselves as the "root" while Christianity represents the "branch"—a secondary or derivative version of the authentic Jewish tradition which was made available and palatable to the Gentile nations. Being antecedent to the birth of the Church gives the Jewish people a sense of priority in covenant. The branch and root figure is transformed into a parent-child relationship or 'mother' and 'daughter.' Abraham Joshua Heschel emphasized the importance of the Jewish-Christian relationship employing precisely this imagery, "Judaism is the mother of the Christian faith. It has a stake in the destiny of Christianity. Should a mother ignore her child, even a wayward, rebellious one?"[12] For Jews or Christians Paul's image of the olive tree, of roots and branches, can provide a framework of interpretation which allows for reconciliation or triumphalism.

Let us turn to our second image created by Franz Rosenzweig—philosopher, theologian, and collaborator with Martin Buber in the translation of the Hebrew Bible into German. Rosenzweig also draws upon the realm of the natural world for his figure of the "star and the rays" to describe the relationship between Judaism and Christianity.

The image is central to Rosenzweig's theological opus, *The Star of Redemption*, written during the years of WWI.[13] Within the context of Rosenzweig's work, the "star" represents the superimposition of six interrelated categories wherein Judaism and Christianity break through the totalizing reality of pagan or philosophical thought: God, Torah, Israel are conjoined with the themes of Creation, Revelation, and Redemption. But with Rosenzweig's presentation of the two communities, it is Judaism which is the core of the star while Christianity represents its rays. In other words, for Rosenzweig, Christianity is illuminated by Judaism:

> The rays of the Star break forth to the exterior, the fire glows toward the interior and neither rests till it has arrived at the end the outermost or the innermost. Both draw everything into the circle filled with their effect. But the rays do so by dividing on the outside scattering, and going their separate ways which only reunite beyond the outer space of the protocosmos when that has been traversed in its entirety.[14]

Both Judaism and Christianity have their place in the world, but according to Rosenzweig, Christianity is called the "eternal way" moving through time. Indeed Christianity is the "master of time."[15] Christianity moves out among the nations and proselytizing. Judaism, by contrast, is not the "eternal way" but the "eternal life" celebrating God through its observance of the sacred festival calendar and obedience to a life of the commandments. Rosenzweig states explicitly that "God withdrew the Jew from this life by arching the bridge to his law high above the current of time which henceforth and to all eternity rushes powerlessly along under its arches."[16] These contrasting descriptions of consciousness about world and time are consistent with the self-understanding ascribed to each community where "Christian consciousness, all steeped in belief, presses toward the beginning of the

way to the first Christian, the crucified one, just as Jewish consciousness, all gathered up in hope presses toward the man of the end of
time, to David's royal sprout.[17]

Star and rays figure Christian "exteriority" in church and state,
while Jewish "interiority" is understood as containing all contradic-
tions within itself. Rosenzweig describes the intensity of this Jewish
interior gaze:

> The flame too flashed in threefold blaze. In three contradictions of
> its own burning life, it internalized the tripartite life of the outer all.
> The might and humility of the Jewish God, the election and the re-
> demptive vocation of Jewish man, the this worldly and eschatologi-
> cal character of the Jewish world—in these three flashes the flame
> gathered mirror like all contradictions into its interior as simple
> contradictions. In contrast to all early flames, it does not simply
> burn out its warmth radiating outward. Rather, because eternally
> feeding on itself, it simultaneously gathers the blaze into its inner-
> most interior as supreme perfervid fire. And by thus gathering its
> blaze inwardly, it in turn smelts the blazing flashing contradictions
> more and more into a unitary still glow.[18]

Ultimately Rosenzweig considers both the Christian eternal way
and the Jewish eternal life to contain complementary dangers to themselves. By radiating apart to the outside, Christianity threatens to lose
itself in individual rays far from the divine nucleus of truth. By glow-
ing toward the inside, Judaism threatened to gather its warmth to its
own bosom, far away from the pagan reality of the world.

These complementary "dangers" set Jew and Christian at eternal
enmity (*Feindschaft*) with one another. The existence of the Jew constantly subjects Christianity to the idea that it is not attaining the goal,
the truth, that it ever remains on the way. In this way Christian hatred
of the Jew, which is heir to the pagan contempt for the Jew, is only self-
hate directed to the "objectionable mute admonisher." Rosenzweig
assures his reader that this "hatred" does not diminish Christians in
the eyes of God. From the divine perspective,

> Jew and Christian both labor at the same task. [God] cannot dis-
> pense with either. He has set enmity between the two for all time

and withal has most intimately bound each to each. To us [Jews] He gave eternal life by kindling the fire of the Star of his truth in our hearts. Them [the Christians] He set on the eternal way by causing them to pursue the rays of that Star of His truth for all time unto the eternal end. We thus espy in our hearts the true image of the Truth, yet on the other hand we turn our backs on temporal life and the life of the times turns away from us. They for their part run after the current of time, but truth remains at their back, though led by it since they follow its rays they do not see it with their eyes.[19]

One might, at this point, presume that Rosenzweig is simply inverting the potential triumphalism of Paul's figure of roots and branches into the image of the star and the rays. Yet he surprises us. He confesses that, "The whole truth belongs neither to them nor to us," which means that neither side can claim a total victory of being "most beloved in God's eyes." Even though the Jews bear the truth within themselves, they must look inside, and though they see the stars, they would not see the rays. The whole truth would demand not on only seeing its light but also what is illuminated by it. Totalizing truth, for Rosenzweig, is beyond the reach of either Jews or Christians. God imparts to us "only what we, as living creatures can bear."[20]

Rosenzweig's compelling image of the star and its rays provides the ground for considerable theological reflection to both Jewish and Christian theologians. His thought shares some dimensions with his contemporaries Leo Baeck and Martin Buber. All three of these scholars were responding to Christian philosophical and theological writings that sought to portray Judaism as legalistic, particular, and inferior to Christianity, which was the more universalistic and compassionate religious community. Buber and Baeck chose to attack Christianity as tied to a romantic aesthetic which rendered it less amenable to ethical commandment and responsibility. Only Rosenzweig created a systematic response to Christian theological arguments within the framework of salvation history. But Rosenzweig's creativity exacts a great price from Judaism and the Jewish people by denying them their proper role in world history. The screaming silence of Jews from the stage of history must be juxtaposed to what occurred shortly after Rosenzweig's death in 1929 with the rise of National Socialism and its

Endlösung (Final Solution), not *Erlösung* (Redemption) for the Jewish people.

Emerging from the nightmare of the Shoa, Jews and Christians are seeking a hermeneutical framework that will provide for their theological reflections which are grounded in historical reality rather than escaping from it, and where they can hear the words of Scripture without competing with each other. In the contemporary world it would seem that neither community will succeed in heeding the divine command to do justice and participate in building the divine sovereignty by seeking refuge in a liturgical calendar lived only with God at the expense of compassionate attention to the human world which has its origin in God. Holiness is to be sought in taking responsibility for how we live out the covenant in the world for ourselves and others.

Out of the void of silence, the images of the tree and the star might however provide a point of embarkation. The images recall the biblical witness of "heaven" and "earth" which are often called upon in the book of Deuteronomy to corroborate the divine command. Let us listen, "I call heaven and earth to witness this day, I have set life and death before you this day, the blessing and the curse—therefore choose life that you and your children might live" (Deut. 30:19). How might Christians and Jews "choose life" together while at the same time nurturing their unique identities?

Gerald Bruns, in his essay "What is Tradition?" provides a daring approach for both communities to approach our traditions.[21] He compares the approach of theologians with hermeneutical philosophers, indicating that for one group the "entry into mystery" is comparable to the other group's entry into the "conflict of interpretations." For Bruns the way into this mystery or conflict is to employ Martin Heidegger's notion of the "rift" as that dif-ference (*Unter-schied*) that holds apart what it calls together. The image of the "rift" is introduced in Heidegger's essay "The Origin of the Work of Art" and refers to the opposition of "earth" and "world," where the latter is formed by humans where they enter into the open through the work of art. The earth withholds itself from the opening of the world and resists "every effort to break into it and bring it under control." Heidegger argues, "The opposition of earth and world is a striving. But we would surely all too easily falsify its nature if we were to confound striving with discord and dispute, and thus see it only as disorder and destruction. In essential striving, rather, the opponents raise each other into the self assertion of their natures. . . . In the struggle each opponent carries the other beyond itself."[22] Indeed according to Heidegger this conflict or rift is not a mere cleft ripped open, rather it is the intimacy with which opponents belong to each other. This rift does not let the opponents break apart, it brings the opposition of measure and boundary into their common outline (*Umriss*).[23]

In their long history of sharing a common text, the Hebrew Bible, Jews and Christians are joined by the rift of interpretive traditions that have been in conflict. Rather than dismissing these interpretive traditions as irrelevant, we might recover a significant element of the oppositional struggle between Jews and Christians in their efforts to appropriate the Scripture. Reading Hebrew Scripture through the lenses of diverging traditions of exegesis is to recapitulate the rift between Jews and Christians in the fullness of its pain. However, it is not exclusively a pain that rends apart; it also draws both Jews and Christians together. Heidegger describes the relationship between the rift and pain in this manner:

> Pain rends. It is the rift. But it does not tear apart into disparate fragments. Pain indeed tears asunder, it separates yet at the same time it draws everything together, gathers it to itself. Its rending, as a separating that gathers is at the same time that drawing which like the pen drawing of a plan or a sketch draws and joins together what is held apart in separation. Pain is the rending that divides and gathers. Pain is the joining of the rift. The joining is the threshold. It settles the between, the middle of the two that are separated in it. Pain joins the rift of difference. Pain is the difference itself.[24]

Bruns then expands Heidegger's idea of the rift suggesting,

> If one maps this Heideggerian design onto the relation of Christianity and Judaism one does not get a typology of testaments but a mutual and painful antagonism that cannot be resolved even by the monumental achievement of doing away with history itself. . . . Judaism is not *Vergangen* but confronts Christianity all along its way

or all the way down as an irrepressible prophetic voice, not the voice of the precursor awaiting final redemption but the voice of the outside still awaiting acknowledgment. From the standpoint of interpretation, this means acknowledgment of a double reading of the Scriptures as well as of history, a reading that calls each side into its own self-assertion but also places each side at risk, always exposing its self-image to alternative descriptions.[25]

Bruns suggests a framework for our common theological reflection which would juxtapose Jewish and Christian readings of the Hebrew Bible as its *foundational* activity. As theologians we would become *Doctores in Sacra Pagina* or *Parshanim,* interpreters of a revelatory text which we have held, presently hold, and ultimately will continue to teach and preach within liturgical and academic settings.

The reframing suggested by the image of the "rift" might bring about a shift in the way we think about Scripture. I believe that taking interpretive activity seriously means a movement from a focus on the world of figure or symbol to greater emphasis upon narrative context—or at least highlighting the narrative context in which the figures are embedded. Paul's olive tree and branches can be read in a paratactic or non-narrative framework, which then delivers the root and branches as severed until the eschaton. Rosenzweig's image of the star and rays can maintain their ambivalent relationship precisely because only the lesser part of the image—the rays—travel through history and the world. The "eternal way" is deprived of its grounding, its nurture, its connection to the earth and the land. In the shadow of the Shoa Jewish and Christian communities can be in self-witnessing juxtaposition to one another—they must no longer accept that their enmity will be resolved only when time, as we know it, comes to an end.

Let me then offer an example of the process of this type of theological reflection. Rather than focusing on an image which, as we have indicated, may be easily removed from its larger narrative context, let us focus on the interpretative traditions of a narrative within the Hebrew Bible—specifically Jacob and Esau. Like other narratives of the early ancestors of biblical Israel, this narrative focuses on how the inheritance of the covenant is transmitted from one generation to the

next. As we move through generations of Jewish and Christian interpreters from the patristic and rabbinic periods through the Middle
Ages until the experience of what Hans Frei has called "the eclipse of
biblical narrative," it is possible to discern how the interpretive traditions fill in the gaps in the narrative to concord with their exclusivist
readings.[26] We might then be able to appreciate how our traditions
have closed the biblical text rather than allowing for the narratives of
Scripture to critique our exegetical perspectives.

For purposes of this essay we shall explore only the Jewish tradition
about Jacob and Esau, the two sons of Isaac who come to represent the
communities of Jews and Christians. In their rereading of this biblical
story, the rabbis and their descendants became tradents of an exclusivist, irreconcilable covenant in which Jacob triumphs and Esau is
always excluded.[27]

From the moment of their conception, the two children of Isaac
and Rebecca are a source of pain. As the children fought in her womb,
Rebecca cried out, "Why should I suffer such agony" (Gen. 25:21).
The divine voice then prophesied that the two children in her womb
were two peoples who would separate one from the other and the
elder would serve the younger. In their exposition of this passage,
the Rabbis point out that the struggling in Rebecca's womb revealed
the character of each child. When Rebecca passed a pagan temple Esau
fought to get out and when she passed a synagogue or house of study
Isaac strove to leave her womb.[28] The rabbinic interpretation of imperial Rome with Christianity and the subsequent efforts in Europe to
revive *Romanum Imperium* provided generations of Jewish interpreters
with the opportunity to mine their condemnations of Esau as a figure
of evil.

This hostility against Christianity may be reflected in the interrup-
tion of the biblical narrative which describes interactions between
Jacob and Esau in Genesis 25:29–30. In the Babylonian Talmud, Trac-
tate Baba Batra 16b, the following tradition is reported in the name of
Rabbi Johanan.

That wicked Esau committed five sins on that day [i.e. the day of
Abraham's death]. He dishonored a betrothed maiden, he committed a murder, he denied God, he denied the resurrection of the

dead and he spurned his birthright. We know that he dishonored a betrothed maiden because it is written "And Esau came in from the field," and it is written in another place, "He found her in the field" (Dt. 22:27). We know that he committed murder because it is written here that he was faint. . . . We know that he denied God because it is written here, "What benefit is this to me?" We know that he denied the resurrection of the dead because he said, "Behold I am about to die," and also that he spurned the birthright because it is written, "so Esau despised his birthright."

The two biblical verses in Genesis describe a series of actions by Jacob and Esau. Jacob was cooking the lentils and Esau came in from the field and he was tired (Gen. 25:30). A dialogue between the two brothers created the transaction that led to the exchange of the birthright for the lentils (Gen. 25:31–34a). Only the closing remark evaluates the interactions between the brothers stating that Esau despised his birthright. Rabbi Johanan's statement transforms Esau into the antithesis of rabbinic virtue: he does not respect the marriage bond, he violates the ten commandments as a murderer, and he denies fundamental rabbinic beliefs in God and the resurrection of the dead. By his behavior Esau is pushed beyond the possibility of reconciliation with his brother.

This pattern of inscribing irreconcilable differences between Jacob and Esau into the biblical text continues in rabbinic expositions of Genesis 26–33. For the Rabbis, because of the birth prophecy of Jacob and Esau, no reconciliation would be possible. However, the biblical narrative of Genesis 32:4–22 challenged this univocal conclusion. Jacob made preparations to meet his brother (Gen. 33:4–6). He had great anxiety about the meeting (Gen. 33:7–9). He offered a petition to God to rescue him (Gen. 33:10–13). As a final precaution, he divided his camp and prepared gifts for his brother (Gen. 33:14–22).

After his solitary experience of wrestling with the angel who changed his name at the river Jabbok, Jacob went to meet Esau. The reconciliation between Jacob and Esau in the biblical text is reinscribed by the Rabbis. Genesis 33:4 states, "Esau ran to greet him. He embraced him and falling on his neck, he kissed him and they wept." However, the Rabbis present the scene as follows:

AND ESAU RAN TO MEET HIM . . . AND KISSED HIM: The letters of the biblical word ["and kissed him"] have dots above them in the written text. Wherever you find the plain writing exceeding the dotted letters, you must interpret the plain writing. If the dotted letters exceed the plain writing, you must interpret the dotted letters. Here the plain writing does not exceed the dotted letters nor do the dotted letters exceed the plain writing. Therefore it teaches that Esau kissed him with sincerity. R. Jannai said to him, "If this is the case why does the word have dots at all? Rather it teaches that Esau wished to bite him, but the patriarch Jacob's neck was turned to marble and that wicked man's teeth were loosened. Hence the Scripture states, "And they wept." One wept because of his neck and the other wept because of his teeth.[29]

An investigation of the rabbinic and medieval commentaries on this passage indicate that they continue the ambivalence toward Esau reflected in this passage. Rashi, Rabbi Solomon b. Isaac of Troyes, whose commentary provides the formative reading of the Pentateuch for traditional Jews even in the contemporary world offers another interpretation: Esau's kiss might have been sincere, but R. Simon b. Yohai claims that Esau was overcome by emotion and kissed Jacob with a whole heart.[30] However, after Rashi subsequent generations favored the interpretation which emphasized the insincerity of Esau.[31]

It is significant that where the biblical text provided an opening toward emotional reconciliation the Rabbis and their successors utilized an orthographic device, the inscription of dots, to emphasize an exegetical anomaly. The reader is pulled visually toward the word which indicates the kiss. However, the commentary is able to excise the action of reconciliation not be denying the act but providing an interpretation of its intention. As they impute evil motives to Esau, they transformed the kiss into an attack. The word for "bit" in Hebrew can be substituted for "kiss" through changing only one letter. For generations of literate Jews, their experience in the diaspora of Christian power was mirrored in their exegetical tradition. It nurtured their image of a deceptive Esau which eclipsed the alternative representation in the Scripture of a brother, overwhelmed emotionally, who embraced his sibling after many years of estrangement. Jacob's neck of marble, provided miraculously by God, could serve as a paradigm of resistance to the hostile gentile environment.

By rereading the biblical text through the interpretive tradition we can observe an example of the Jewish response to the question of *Verus Israel*. Read synoptically with the Christian tradition on Jacob and Esau, the Jewish re-narrantization becomes an image of the rift that binds—a counter-narrative which provides a prophylaxis against disenfranchisement and exile.

As the new millennium stretches before us, Jews and Christians are gaining increasing knowledge of the rift that binds them together. An archeology of our traditions that looks only to the variety of influences at the beginnings of the Church and synagogue cannot fully provide a corrective norm for our mutual explorations of how we might care for one another. In the presence of one another we can look through layer after layer of our interpretive traditions of the text we hold in common. We need to concede the fundamental lens which animates our interpretation: Christ for the Christian community; the collectivity of the oral Torah for rabbinic Judaism. However, what the violence of the past millennium does demand is that we look to the Hebrew Scriptures for the key to our mutual bond of community and non-community. To diminish its role makes us deaf to the divine call to choose life for our communities and for one another.

Notes

1. There is a considerable bibliography on Jewish-Christian relations in the U.S. See Michael Shermis, ed., *Jewish-Christian Relations: An Annotated Bibliography and Resource Guide* (Bloomington, Ind., 1988).

2. Michael A. Signer, "*Communitas et Universitas: From Theory to Practice in Jewish Christian Relations*," in J. Petuchowski, ed., *When Jews and Christians Meet* (Albany, N.Y., 1989), 59–86.

3. Abraham Joshua Heschel, "No Religion Is an Island," in Susannah Heschel, ed., *Moral Grandeur and Spiritual Audacity: Essays of Abraham Joshua Heschel* (New York, 1996), 286–87.

4. The leitmotif of "being for the Other" may be found throughout the works of Levinas, but in *Difficult Freedom: Essays on Judaism* (Baltimore, 1990) one can discover its application within a specifically Jewish framework. The

move from experience to interpretation is an expansion of a theological method proposed by David Tracy in *The Analogical Imagination: Christian Theology and the Culture of Pluralism* (New York, 1978) and Peter Ochs in *The Return to Scripture in Judaism and Christianity: Essays in Postcritical Scriptural Interpretation* (New York, 1993). It is utilized most effectively by Levinas himself in *Nine Talmudic Readings* (Bloomington, Ind., 1990).

5. Walter Benjamin, "The Theory of Knowledge, Theory of Progress," in G. Smith, ed., *Benjamin: Philosophy, Aesthetics, History* (Chicago, 1989), 49. A more fully grounded philosophical anthropology of the image is provided by Hans Jonas in his essay, "Tool, Image, and Grave: On What Is Beyond the Animal in Man?" in Lawrence Vogel, ed., *Mortality and Morality: A Search for the Good after Auschwitz* (Evanston, Ill., 1996) 75–86.

6. The translation and many of the ideas in this section of the paper derive from Joseph A. Fitzmyer, *Romans: A New Translation with Introduction and Commentary*, Anchor Bible Ser., vol. 33 (New York, 1993), especially pp. 539–632.

7. J. A. Fitzmyer, *Romans*, 616: "Throughout the argument based on the wild olive shoot Paul implies that the lopped-off natural branches have not yet been cast on the rubbish heap. Israel has not been definitively rejected by God (11:1). The 'power' of which Paul speaks must be understood as that related to the gospel (1:16), the 'power for salvation.' Hence Israel's salvation cannot take place apart from the power manifested in the preaching of the gospel of Christ."

8. E. Fisher and L. Klenicki, eds., *John Paul II on Jews and Judaism* (Washington, D.C., 1987).

9. Krister Stendahl, *Paul among the Jews and Gentiles* (Philadelphia, 1984); Paul van Buren, *A Theology of the Jewish-Christian Reality*, 3 vols, (New York, 1980–84).

10. J. A. Fitzmeyer, *Romans*, 618-620.

11. W. Seiferth, *Synagogue and Church in the Middle Ages: Two Symbols in Art and Literature* (New York, 1970).

12. Abraham Joshua Heschel, "No Religion Is an Island," 242.

13. Franz Rosenzweig, *The Star of Redemption,* trans. William Hallo (New York, 1970); rpt. Notre Dame, Ind., 1985). Most of the passages in this essay will be cited according to the pagination of Fritz A. Rothschild, *Jewish Perspectives on Christianity* (New York, 1990), who utilized Hallo's translation of the *Star,* 336–53 and 395–417.

14. F. Rothschild, *Jewish Perspectives,* 206–7.

15. Ibid., 191.

16. Ibid., 190.

17. Ibid., 198.

18. Ibid., 211.

19. Ibid.

20. Ibid., 225.

21. Gerald L. Bruns, *Hermeneutics: Ancient and Modern* (New Haven, 1992), 195–212.

22. Bruns, *Hermeneutics*, 206–7, quoting M. Heidegger, *Poetry, Language, Thought*, trans. Albert Hofstadter (New York, 1971), 49.

23. Bruns, *Hermeneutics*, 207; Heidegger, *Poetry*, 63.

24. Bruns, *Hermeneutics*, 207–8; Heidegger, *Poetry*, 204.

25. Bruns, *Hermeneutics*, 208.

26. Hans W. Frei, *The Eclipse of Biblical Narrative* (New Haven, 1974). David Tracy, *The Analogical Imagination*, provides a framework for theological reflection within a narrative framework.

27. Beginning with Romans 9:11–13 the Christian tradition reversed the favored status of the Jewish people, identifying Jacob with the Church and Esau with the Jews. Jon Levenson, *The Death and Resurrection of the Beloved Son* (New Haven, 1993) treats this motif from the Bible through early Jewish and Christian interpretation.

28. Genesis Rabbah 63.

29. Genesis Rabbah 78:12.

30. Rabbi Solomon b. Isaac of Troyes, Commentary on Genesis 33:4.

31. See Menahem Kasher, *Torah Shelemah* (Jerusalem, 1992), 1301, n. 15.

EIGHT

The Unity We Still Seek:
An Eastern Orthodox Perspective

Thomas Hopko

∞

All Eastern Orthodox churches, except the Orthodox Church of
Georgia, and all Oriental Orthodox churches are members of the
World Council of Churches and participate in the ecumenical movement.[1] All have grave difficulties with ecumenism, some of which, but
certainly not all, are due to misunderstanding and misinformation.
And all have in them strong voices calling for a complete cessation of
ecumenical activity.

What follows is an interpretation and assessment of Orthodox participation in the ecumenical movement, particularly the search for
unity among Christian churches, by an Orthodox sympathetic to ecumenism as traditionally understood and engaged by the Orthodox.
While the paper is my own, I believe that it generally represents the
position of those in the Orthodox Church who remain convinced that
ecumenical activity is an essential part of Christian faith and life in the
modern world.

The unity which Christians of apostolic tradition still seek for their
churches is Jesus Christ's unity with God his Father in the Holy Spirit.
According to Saint John's Gospel, Jesus prayed for this unity for his
Apostles and for those who would believe in him through their word.[2]

He prayed for this unity so that the world might know and believe that the God who loves and sends him also loves those whom he sends, and those who believe through their teaching. All creation is made for this divine unity. Israel, God's first-born Son, bears it to the nations. Jesus, the Messiah, is crucified and glorified that it may be accomplished. The Holy Spirit is given that it may be fulfilled.

Christ's unity with God the Father in the Holy Spirit, which is eternally actualized in the Godhead, is manifested on earth where God acts through his Word and Spirit with his creatures, whether or not they consciously know it. This unity is being realized where men and women strive for truth, love, justice, peace, beauty, joy . . . and all the divine qualities for which they are made in God's image and likeness. To the measure that human beings seek God's perfection and cooperate with God's grace, knowingly or unknowingly, there will be unity, communion, and life. To the degree that they doubt and deny their divine destiny, there is division and death.

From an Orthodox Christian perspective, God has already united all things in Christ. He has already made his Son the head over all things for the Church. This is God's plan from before the foundation of the ages. It is the "mystery of Christ," hidden from the angels and made known in the Church which, according to apostolic testimony, is the Israel of God, Christ's body and bride, the temple of the Holy Spirit, the pillar and bulwark of the truth, the fulness of him who fills all in all.[3] The sole reason for the Church's being is to make Christ's unity with God in the Spirit as knowable and accessible to humanity as is now possible on earth until Jesus returns in glory to establish divine unity in the universe.

The Church, as Father Alexander Schmemann would say, is not an organization with a gospel; it is a Gospel with organizations. It is not an institution with mysteries; it is a Mystery with institutions. Church unity, in this perspective, is unity in the Gospel of God and the Mystery of Christ as revealed, known, proclaimed, celebrated and witnessed in the formal ecclesial doctrines, sacramental structures, and liturgical rites of the Christian churches. In this perspective, Church unity has virtually nothing to do with theological systems, church politics, popular pieties, or holy people. It has only to do with the formal faith, order, and worship of the churches *qua* churches. It is about what the churches of Christ, as Christ's one holy Church, believe, teach, pray, and do.[4]

Theologians and theologians come and go. So do ecclesiastical policies and actions, and pietistic devotions and practices. Some are formally received and canonized, thereby becoming part of the Church's divine humanity in history. Others are dismissed and forgotten. Still others produce factions and divisions, schisms and heresies. Righteous people, some graced with extraordinary sanctity, are found everywhere; within the churches and without. God is not bound. His divine Word, incarnate as Jesus, fashions everyone and everything. His quickening Spirit, everywhere present, blows where he wills. The Lord acts in and with all of his creatures according to their willingness and ability to cooperate with his divine energies. God builds communion and unity wherever, however, and in whomever he can.

We can say these things, from an Orthodox perspective, and claim to know that they are true, because we believe that God also acts personally and directly within human history through his divine Word and Spirit in his chosen people. He founds his new and final covenant community with his creatures on faith in his Son, Jesus, the Messiah of Israel, so that the fulness of grace and truth, the fulness of unity and communion, the fulness of life and beatitude, and, indeed, the whole fulness of the Godhead itself may be fully present and consciously known by all human beings, from the least to the greatest, who believe and are baptized. God establishes his Church and acts within it so that he may truly be "all and in all" for those who know and love him, or who rather are known and loved by him, in Jesus Christ and the Holy Spirit.[5]

The unity which apostolic Christians still seek for the churches is the unity which is actualized wherever God acts among creatures. It is the communion with God which is consciously known and experienced by Christian saints. It is the Church's unity in faith, order, and worship which, according to the Acts of the Apostles, is finally and fully given to Jesus' disciples on the day of Pentecost following the Lord's Pascha. This unity, ideally portrayed in the book of Acts, did not long exist among all who claimed to be disciples of Christ, if, indeed, it ever so existed in history. According to the Christian Scriptures, controversies and disputes about Jesus existed among the various Jewish parties and the first Gentile Christians from the very beginning, with the factions and divisions, schisms and heresies, which were, according to Saint Paul (himself a disputed figure), inevitable and even necessary "so that the genuine among you may be recognized" (*ina oi dokimoi phaneroi genontai en hymin*).[6] Indeed all the writings of the New Testament canon reflect divisions among Christians from the very start. The first letter attributed to the apostle John testifies to this in the simple sentence:

> They went out from us, but they were not of us; for if they had been of us, they would have continued with us; but they went out, that it might be plain that they all are not of us [*ina phanerothosin oti ouk eisin pantes ex hemon*].[7]

Orthodox Christians believe that the "genuine" who preserve and maintain the unity of the Church are those who are tested and approved. They are the "called and chosen and faithful."[8] They are the believing baptized men and women who have "continued steadfastly in the apostle's doctrine, and the communion, the breaking of the bread and the prayer."[9] They are the fathers, mothers, saints, and martyrs of every age and generation—always few and always persecuted—who, with the faithful bishops in apostolic succession, believe the gospel (*evangelion*), receive the tradition (*paradosis*), and guard the deposit (*paratheke*) of the Church in ways befitting the mystery of God's unity for the whole of creation in Christ and the Spirit.[10]

Eastern Orthodox Christians believe that the Church's God-given unity—which is the unity still to be sought by the separated and divided churches—has been faithfully kept and developed in Christian history only in the Orthodox churches of Nicene and Chalcedonian faith and tradition, which follow the canonized writings of the New Testament and the teachings of the Apostolic Fathers received by the early Church. We consider the doctrine, order, and worship of all other Christian churches to be in some ways untrue, misleading, incomplete, or inaccurate.

Confessing our sins and admitting our failures, both personal and corporate, members of the Orthodox churches participate in ecumenical activity in order to witness to this conviction about the Church and the churches, and to work to overcome the disagreements and divisions among the separated bodies, while cooperating in all ways possible in the state of disagreement and division. We strive to identify and affirm what is good, true, right, and beautiful, as we understand these divine realities, wherever they are found, within the churches and without. And we rejoice to recognize the "vestiges of the Church" wherever they be, with the genuine expressions of Christian teaching, sacramental life, sanctity, and service which the Lord inspires in the churches that we cannot completely identify as Christ's holy Church. We try according to our ability and strength to cooperate with everyone as we can, without betraying "God's Gospel" as we understand it, and without compromising "the faith once for all delivered to the saints" as we believe it to be received, guarded, elaborated, and handed on, without error or change, in the Orthodox Church.[11]

Orthodox Christians involved in ecumenical activity believe that significant progress has been made in many ways in this ecumenical century. We think that we are better able than ever before to distinguish between what is essential and non-essential in Christian life and teaching; to identify and affirm acceptable variations in teachings and practices; to assess and evaluate what used to be called the "non-theological factors" effecting church unity; and to work with greater insight and clarity to overcome substantial disagreements and differences in the churches' formal faith, order, and worship.

In doctrinal articulation, for example, such progress has been reached on the understanding of the unity of divinity and humanity in the person of God's incarnate Son and Word, Jesus Christ, that official meetings of bishops and theologians of the anti-Chalcedonian Oriental churches and the pro-Chalcedonian Eastern churches have agreed that this christological issue is no longer an obstacle to full eucharistic communion between our long-separated churches. What remains now, our leaders tell us, are the difficult tasks of coordinating liturgical worship, establishing appropriate organizational structures, healing painful memories, and convincing the fulness of the churches' members to accept contemporary interpretations of the writings of the teachers historically involved in the controversy without cursing anyone or anything from the past. Without success in such healing and reconciling efforts, which can only come by God's grace and our willingness to refer all judgment on those outside the Church to God alone, the common understanding now achieved about the person of Christ will not be sufficient to bring these separated churches into full sacramental communion and unity.[12]

Progress has also been achieved between Eastern and Western churches concerning the understanding of the Holy Spirit's eternal procession from God the Father. Virtually all agree on the need to remove the *filioque* from the Nicene-Constantinopolitan creed, or at least to explain it in a way acceptable to Orthodoxy without insisting on its inclusion in the creed, with the explanation which was until quite recently required by the Western (and Eastern) churches using the symbol.[13] But here too there must be a healing of memories and a willingness to allow for the churches to interpret the past in ways that permit them to retain their convictions without rejecting a contemporary agreement in doctrine which all can now honestly claim.

Progress has also been made in understanding Christ's mother Mary as Theotokos; and in explaining her conception, dormition, birthgiving, and place in Christian life and worship in ways other than those determined by the dogmatic statements of the Roman Church on these issues, together with the anthropology, hamartology, and soteriology on which these official dogmas were originally based. There are also encouraging changes regarding Mary in Protestant churches which formerly excluded Christ's mother from their faith, worship, and spiritual life, and even from ecumenical discussion itself.[14]

Progress has also been made in recent decades in understanding the Church as a communal body in which all members have their proper place and ministry. Probably more has been written by contemporary Orthodox thinkers about the nature and task of the Church than on any other subject. And greater clarification has probably been achieved on this issue with and among Christians in the West, notwithstanding the unresolved differences and disagreements, than on any other. This seems to be particularly true with regard to the relationship between Scripture and tradition, authority and freedom, hierarchy and collegiality, governance and ministry, and the communion of local churches as each itself being, and all in communion comprising, Christ's one catholic Church.

Generally speaking also, the documents of the Second Vatican Council of the Roman Catholic Church (if not the so-called "spirit of Vatican II" and much that was done invoking this "spirit"), though far from perfect from an Orthodox perspective, are certainly more acceptable to Orthodoxy than the teachings of Vatican I, or the councils of Trent or Florence. The ecclesiastical order and liturgical rituals that accompany and actualize the statements of Vatican II are also in many ways more acceptable to the Orthodox than the old Roman practices. This is particularly true about teachings and actions having to do with the church and salvation, baptism and eucharist, and the relation of the Roman Church to other Christian churches, particularly the Orthodox, and, we may also say, the Eastern rite churches united with Rome. Words of praise and hope are also in order with regard to the new *Catechism of the Catholic Church* which presents and explains Christian doctrine on many issues in ways wholly acceptable to Orthodoxy.

Similar positive things can and indeed must be said from an Orthodox perspective about the work of the Faith and Order Commission of the World Council of Churches. The WCC Faith and Order documents *Baptisms, Eucharist and Ministry*,[15] for example, and *Confessing the One Faith: An Ecumenical Explication of the Apostolic Faith as It Is Confessed in the Nicene-Constantinopolitan Creed (381)*,[16]—with the many different studies that went into the production of these documents and followed their publication—and the changes which they effected in doctrinal teaching, liturgical worship, ecclesiastical polity, and spiritual life in many churches of Reformed traditions can only be welcomed and praised from an Orthodox perspective.

These positive achievements, and many others, have somewhat tempered the "Orthodox agony" in the ecumenical movement lamented by Fr. Alexander Schmemann almost forty years ago.[17] The discrepancies he describes between "official" Orthodoxy and the "average" Orthodox in regard to ecumenism, and between what the Orthodox Church actually is in contrast to how it is presented at ecumenical meetings, are certainly not less today than they were then. What seems to be very different, however, is that the "Western presuppositions" which once reigned in the ecumenical movement as a Western, primarily Protestant enterprise, are no longer in place, and ecumenical agencies such as the World Council of Churches are no longer virtually the only organs for ecumenical activity as they once were. This means that the Orthodox can now "participate" in a great variety of ecumenical activities, and not merely be "represented" in a few official organizations, as Fr. Schmemann described it. It also means that they can exercise considerable impact on ecumenical activity if they choose to do so. This does not mean that the Orthodox will cease to be a minority in the ecumenical arena, often compelled to protest against majority decisions and actions. Still less does it mean that they will easily convince others in the ecumenical movement of the truths of Orthodoxy. But it does mean that the Orthodox today need not necessarily participate in ecumenical work according to someone else's rules, or simply be spectators at someone else's activity and, from time to time, make separate statements about that activity without much effect, or even attention. The real question today, however, is whether or not the Orthodox churches have the will, energy, and resources to participate in ecumenical activity at all, given what is happening in their churches, in other churches, and in the world as a whole.[18]

Whatever hopes may exist with regard to the quest for church unity among Orthodox Christians, old obstacles continue to stand in the way of achieving the unity we still seek for the churches from an Orthodox perspective, and new obstacles have arisen which appear to render the accomplishment of full communion in faith, order, and worship among the churches more unlikely than ever before.

The fundamental difficulty for church unity which critically effects all issues and aspects of ecumenical activity designed to promote the reunion of divided churches is that of determining the formal authoritative position of a given church in matters of faith, order, and worship. Seventy years ago at the First World Conference on Faith and Order in Lausanne, thirty-five years ago at the opening of the Second Vatican Council in Rome, and even twenty-five years ago at the founding of the Ecumenical Study Center here in Tantur, it was relatively easy to determine what the various ecclesial communions and confessional families believed and practiced. Their faith was clearly expressed in their confessional statements, ecclesiastical structures, and corporate worship services. This is no longer the case.

Regarding the Roman Catholic Church, for example, the church's position is still clear on papal infallibility and the pope's episcopal jurisdiction over all church members, including the other bishops, based on a particular interpretation of Peter's role in the early church and the pope as his unique successor. The bishop of Rome still claims and exercises special prerogatives in defining Christian doctrine and morals, and special rights over the bishops of all other churches whom he continues to appoint, and whose episcopal authority still depends on their union with him, and obedience to him, based on his "Petrine" powers.

It is also still clear that the Orthodox Church considers this Roman teaching and practice unacceptable to Christian faith and life for exegetical, theological, and historical reasons (and not merely because of "Eastern" customs and traditions); and finds it incompatible with the Gospel of God, the mystery of Christ, and the unity which God gives to his Church in his Son and Spirit. For the Orthodox—however much we realize the need for ecclesial leadership, order, and witness on a worldwide level, and lament the confusion which now reigns among Christians in this area—the conviction still holds that every bishop who receives the laying-on of hands in apostolic faith, tradition, and historical succession, confessing Jesus as "the Christ, the Son of the living God," is a successor of Peter and the Apostles, none of whom were bishops of local churches. Each such bishop is ordained to guarantee in his sacramental person and ministry the unity, identity, integrity, solidarity, and continuity of the faith and life of Christ's Church. And each is called and consecrated to exercise fully the sacramental service of rightly handling the word of truth, binding and loosing, and feeding the flock of Jesus within the communion of baptized believers.[19]

In general, even with the many positive recent changes, the organization and operation of the Vatican continues to provide stumbling blocks on the path to Church unity from an Orthodox perspective. Obstructive issues for the Orthodox range from the manner in which Rome decides and enforces official church doctrine and discipline to the way bishops are assigned and saints are canonized, to teachings and practices on marriage, divorce, and celibacy, to Roman Catholic activities in regions where Orthodox leadership has been gravely weakened and church life all but totally destroyed by communist regimes.

A new thing in the Roman Church today which presents new difficulties in the quest for church unity from an Orthodox perspective is the fact that bishops and priests, as well as men and women in religious orders, (not to speak of the laity), are known to confess convictions and condone practices contrary to the church's official teachings, including that of the papacy itself. Dissension is sometimes carried to the point of violating the ancient ecclesial principle that the Church's "rule of faith" (*regula fidei*), its "law of believing" (*lex credendi*), and its "law of worship" (*lex orandi*), each affirm and establish the other in a unified witness to the one Gospel. This makes it difficult to determine exactly what it now means to be Roman Catholic, and allows it to be said, only partially in jest, that the only requirement seems to be the willingness to continue to participate in a church united with Rome. Because of this, not a few Orthodox think that an Orthodox church would be quickly and easily received into communion with Rome today with virtually no other condition than that of formally accepting the pope as its leader.

When it comes to the churches of the Anglican and Reformed traditions, the ability for us Orthodox to determine what a given communion officially stands for today is extremely difficult because of the great variety of doctrines, orders, and forms of worship which appear to be acceptable in these churches, whatever is formally voted by their respective administrative and judicial organs. Old difficulties concerning scripture, tradition, doctrine, sacraments, and ministry, where significant progress seems to have been made in some areas, are now becoming confused by new teachings and practices in these churches. This is especially true on issues regarding gender and sexuality, the uniqueness of Jesus, and the relationship of God, Christ, the Spirit, and the Church to non-Christian peoples and spiritual traditions.

Debates and disagreements on these issues have produced a host of new difficulties about the canon, authority and interpretation of the Bible, the place of the ancient councils and canons, and the significance of Church Tradition. They effect the teachings and practices of the churches with regard to the naming of God, the baptismal formula, the use of the Lord's Prayer, and the understanding of the Trinity, as well as the understanding of marriage and family, homosexuality, the ordination of women, and the requirements for ordination and participation in sacraments generally. They also effect the ways in which the churches understand and practice mission and evangelism, and explain and relate to the saving activity of God through Christ and the Holy Spirit outside the Christian Church.

Generally speaking, the greatest obstacle to church unity in the area of "order" still seems to be the understanding in all the churches—Orthodox, Roman, Anglican, and Reformed—about how the priesthood of the ordained ministers relates to the unique highpriesthood of Jesus and to the priesthood of all who are baptized in Christ and sealed by his Spirit. As the responses to *Baptism, Eucharist and Ministry* demonstrated, the apparent agreements on baptism and eucharist were revealed as more verbal than real when the disagreements still existing in the churches regarding ministry were disclosed.[20] And these differences, including those concerning the churches' sacramental structures generally, seem less likely to be overcome today, especially when we consider the changes in the churches' teachings and practices in the fifteen years since Lima which still continue.

What may happen, however, is that a new alignment of Christians and Christian churches may occur over these controverted and disputed issues, with new divisions in old churches providing a way for new agreements and unions among once-separated believers and ecclesial bodies. With God—and his "unsearchable judgments" and "inscrutable judgments" and "inscrutable ways"—all things are possible.[21] And nothing should be too surprising for those who believe in a Messianic Lord who is born of a virgin, made perfect through suffering, enters his glory by dying, unites all things by being rejected, and asks if he will find faith on earth when he returns to establish God's reign in the universe.[22]

Despite the many painful disagreements and divisions in the Orthodox Church today due to the historical tragedies of recent centuries, particularly the one now ending, Orthodox Christians are convinced that their churches have maintained a doctrine, structure, and liturgy which can still be defended as fitting, proper, and adequate to the God-given unity of the Christian Church.

All Orthodox churches have their relativists who consider Orthodoxy as nothing but their peculiar tribal religion. We also have our zealots, including those who (as in Saint Paul's time) do not always act "according to knowledge" and thereby replace God's righteousness with their own.[23] We also have sectarians in various uncanonical groups who, with some church members, consider ecumenism as a modern heresy. And we have our hypocrites and sinners, with our martyrs and saints. Theological, ecclesiological, liturgical, and canonical controversies abound in all Orthodox churches, with disputes and divisions of personal, political, nationalistic, and ethnic nature. But with all this, and despite it all, the Orthodox churches continue to recognize each other as Christ's one, holy Church by maintaining essential unity within and among themselves in doctrine, order, liturgy, spirituality, discipline, and historical memory and identity.

With many doubts, hesitations, and temptations, all Orthodox churches, with the recent exception of the Georgian Church, also continue to participate in ecumenical activity. Their leaders and faithful members remain ready to affirm God's presence and action wherever it may be; to rejoice in all genuine elements of the Church's apostolic faith, order, and worship, with true teaching, service, and sanctity, wherever they are found; and to cooperate with everyone to the measure that they can. They also consider themselves bound to reject all formal and institutional deviations from sound Christian doctrine, right Christian worship, and proper Christian morality wherever they believe these to be, with perpetual controversy about these issues among themselves.

The Orthodox churches have managed to do this through decades, and in some cases even centuries, of the most relentless and cruel persecution and suffering. And they continue to do so even when they cannot agree among themselves about such things as how their bishops should be elected and consecrated; or how their primates should be seated when they meet in council; or how their churches outside traditionally Orthodox ecclesiastical territories should be established and governed; or how the Ecumenical Patriarch of Constantinople should exercise his ministry of primacy in the modern world; or how they should participate in ecumenical activity.

But be all these things, and many others, as they may, the seeking and striving "that all may be one" in Christ's one, holy Church remains, in an Orthodox perspective, an essential element of Christian faith and life. To refuse to witness to Christ's unity with God, the unity of all creation in Christ, and the unity of Christ's holy Church is a betrayal of Christ and a blasphemy of the Holy Spirit. For the Lord who prayed and gave his life for the union of all,[24] sending his Holy Spirit to call all to unity,[25] has taught us to do the same. After washing the feet of his Apostles at the supper, including those of the one who betrayed him, Jesus said to them and to us: "Truly, truly, I say to you, a servant is not greater than his master, nor is he who is sent greater than he who sent him. If you know these things, blessed are you if you do them."[26]

Notes

1. Eastern Orthodox churches are the Chalcedonian churches in the Byzantine tradition. Oriental Orthodox churches are those which do not accept the council of Chalcedon: Armenian, Coptic, Ethiopian, and Syrian Orthodox. The Orthodox Church of Georgia announced its withdrawal from the WCC and from the European Council of Churches on May 27, 1997.

2. John 17:1–26.

3. Cf. Rom. 11; Gal. 6; 1 Cor. 3, 6, 12; 1 Tim. 3; Eph. 1, 4; Rev. 21.

4. See Georges Florovsky, "Primitive Tradition and the Traditions," in William S. Morris, ed., *The Unity We Seek. Lectures on the Church and the Churches* (Toronto, 1962).

5. 1 Cor. 15:28; Col. 3:11.

6. 1 Cor. 11:19.

7. 1 John 2:19.

8. Rev. 18:14.

9. Acts 2:42.

10. 2 Thess. 2:15, 3:6; 1 Tim. 6:20.

11. Rom. 1:1; Jude 3.

12. "Communique of the Joint Commission of the Theological Dialogue between the Orthodox Church and the Oriental Orthodox Churches (Anba Bishoy Monastery, Egypt, 20–24 June 1989)," *Greek Orthodox Theological Review* 34 (Winter 1989): 393–97; Thomas Fitzgerald, "Toward the Re-establishment of Full Communion: The Orthodox-Orthodox Oriental Dialogue," *Greek Orthodox Theological Review* 36 (Summer 1991), 169–82; "Joint-

Commission of the Theological Dialogue between the Orthodox Church and the Oriental Orthodox Churches (Orthodox Centre of the Ecumenical Patriarchate, Geneva, September 23–28, 1990)," *Greek Orthodox Theological Review* 36 (Summer 1991) 183–88; "Joint Commission of the Theological Dialogue between the Orthodox Church and the Oriental Orthodox Churches (Orthodox Centre of the Ecumenical Patriarchate, Geneva, November 2–6, 1993)" Negative reactions to the work of the joint commission have been expressed in the *Memorandum of the Sacred Community of the Holy Mountain (Mt. Athos) Concerning the Dialogue between the Orthodox and the Anti-Chalcedonian Churches.* (Karyai, 1995); and in *The Ethiopian Orthodox Tewahido Church: Faith, Order of Worship and Ecumenical Relations*, 106–8.

13. The papal encyclical *Dominum et Vivificantem* (1986), does not mention the *filioque*. The new *Catechism of the Catholic Church* (1994) includes the *filioque* in the creed and affirms and justifies it for the "Latin" and "Western" tradition" (246–48), but does not mention it in the section "I believe in the Holy Spirit" (683–747). See also "The Greek and Latin Traditions regarding the Procession of the Holy Spirit," *L'Osservatore Romano* (September 20, 1995).

14. In the new *Catechism of the Catholic Church* the brief explanations which quote the official dogmatic pronouncements on the "immaculate conception" and "assumption" of the Virgin Mary sadly remain unacceptable to Orthodoxy. More happy is the fact that Father Bulgakov would not be ruled out of order today as he was in Lausanne in 1927 for attempting to introduce Mary into ecumenical discussion.

15. (Geneva, 1982). See also *Baptism, Eucharist and Ministry 1982–1990, Report on the Process and Responses* (Geneva, 1990), and *Orthodox Perspectives on BEM* (Brookline, 1985).

16. (Geneva, 1991).

17. See Alexander Schmemann, "Orthodox Agony in the World Council," *Christianity Today*, January 20, 1958, 3–4. Also "Moment of Truth for Orthodoxy," in *Unity in Mid-Career: An Ecumenical Critique* (New York, 1963), and "The Ecumenical Agony," *Church, World, Mission* (Crestwood, 1979).

18. See George Lemopoulos, ed., *The Ecumenical Movement, the Churches and the World Council of Churches: An Orthodox Contribution to the Reflection Process on "The Common Understanding and Vision of the WCC"* (Geneva and Bialystok, 1996), and Todor Sabev, *The Orthodox Churches in the World Council of Churches* (Geneva and Bialystok, 1996).

19. 2 Tim. 2:15; John 20:22 and 21:15–19, which in patristic commentaries is consistently referred to as Peter's reinstatement as chief Apostle after his three denials. See John Meyendorff, ed., *The Primacy of Peter: Essays in Ecclesiology and the Early Church* (Crestwood, N.Y., 1992). Also John Erickson, "Collegiality and Primacy in Orthodox Ecclesiology," in John Erickson, ed., *The Challenge of Our Past: Studies in Orthodox Law and Church History* (Crest-

wood, 1991). Thomas Hopko, "On Ecclesial Conciliarity," in John Breck and J. Meyendorff, eds., *The Legacy of St. Vladimir: Byzantium, Russia, America* (Crestwood, 1990).

20. Thomas Hopko, "Ministry and the Unity of the Church," *St. Vladimir's Theological Quarterly*, 34 (1990).

21. Rom. 11:33, Matt. 19:26, et. al.

22. Luke 18:8.

23. Rom. 10:2.

24. "For the peace from above, for the welfare of the holy churches of God, and for the union of all, let us pray to the Lord" (Byzantine Liturgy).

25. "When the Most High came down and confused the tongues he divided the nations; but when He distributed the tongues of fire He called all to unity. Therefore, with one voice we glorify the all-holy Spirit" (Byzantine Kontakion of Pentecost).

26. John 13:16–17.

NINE

Towards an Ecumenical Ecclesiology of Communion

Jean M. R. Tillard, O. P.

∞

This is a very ambitious and very difficult subject which I have been given. In fact, since the reactions to the Lima document[1] and since the publication of what has come to be known as the *Canberra Statement*,[2] much water has flown under the bridges. Confessionalisms have woken up and have reacted against a certain relativism which seemed to them to be dangerous to faith.[3] In order to complete projects of union, important churches have felt it necessary to qualify or suspend, at least for a certain time, some of their strongest convictions.[4] Recent "consultations" have shown that some church families are incapable of agreeing on the nature of the episcopate, on the relation between the *épiscopè* and *épiscopos*. Are we back with the rock of Sisyphus?

However, a pessimistic view of the situation would be pointless. A huge and deep web has slowly been woven, of ecclesial solidarities, of determinations to seek unity, of brotherhoods re-established, of impatience when faced with the slowness of ecumenical steps, and of "holy anger" with unfortunate decisions. No Penelope could undo it again completely, in secret and in the night of our tribulations since we know beyond a doubt that it was the Spirit of God who has woven it. Against this background, and not in the abstract, we must think of an ecumenical ecclesiology of *communion*. That is the aim of this study.

I. The Starting Point for an Ecumenical Ecclesiology.

Let us define straight away, in order to avoid misunderstandings, that by "ecumenical ecclesiology"—the expression suggested by the organizers of this conference—we understand an ecclesiology based on the attainments of the last decades. We are going to try to uncover a bit in this ecumenical study what we shall call an "ecclesiology in gestation."

An introductory statement seems to us essential. The starting point for this ecclesiology has obviously to be nothing less than a more profound understanding of the work of *God's* grace, as it takes shape in *God's* Church. One cannot speak of the Church before first speaking about grace. I dare to say—even if I provoke some raised eyebrows— that one cannot even speak about Christ as Head of the Church before speaking about grace. For, historically, the event of Jesus Christ stands at the zenith of a large *οἰκονομία* of grace, working *jam ab Abel justo*. In fact, it is important to show the visible Church not as one which manages and channels the grace of God but as one which only finds here identity when encompassed and held by this grace.

This must not be seen as an empty formula. In order to demonstrate its relevance, let us pose some apparently commonplace but really highly pertinent questions. Why, when religions without institutional structures are enjoying such an extraordinary growth, even in the West where they are attracting people "touched by God," are the Christian churches plunging into such a deep crisis? Why is it that, whilst the attitudes and doctrines of these religious groups provoke barely a protest from public opinion, the slightest blunder of the churches in the same areas provokes such radical and severe reactions? Why, since the figure of Christ Jesus still arouses interest, even in the media, is the Christianity of the churches being rejected and sometimes openly scoffed at? When everywhere religiosity and the irrational are coming back strongly, why has the truly supernatural dimension of Christianity so little impact?

It seems to us that, after due reflection, we can only honestly answer these questions by another question, clear but put without aggression. Do the churches not appear, more or less consciously, to keep grace locked up within their structures, their categories, and their institutional frontiers? To the eyes of the secular world, this only makes their divisions worse. The answer seems to us evident. And it will have to guide all ecclesiological thinking.

There is no authentic ecclesiology, capable of gathering the separated churches together in truth, except the one which makes them all cling to the assurance that, because Christ is their head, they are all gathered up in what Irenaeus called "the two hands of God," the Son and the Spirit. However, Son and Spirit transcend them and mold them in a communion with the Father which aims beyond them, to the whole of God's plan. The "recognition" of this radical dependence on the Father and of this insertion into the whole of his plan—which precedes all other considerations of faith and structures (Faith and Order)—places the Church in full harmony with the revelation of the Gospel. In fact, in Jesus Christ it unveils for us that God's plan for humankind is being realized on three levels. They are the liberation of humankind from physical and spiritual misery, the healing of the wounds of desire and freedom, and the association of human destiny (both personal and collective) with the communion of the life of the Trinity. But these levels intersect.

First of all, the Church of God seems to be there. That defines her nature. She is the *pars humanitatis* which, having heard the Good News of God's plan and its realization in Jesus Christ, and having "received" it by understanding its meaning and its implications, lets itself be "grasped" by this grace of God, and lives accordingly. On this way she is *creatura Verbi et Spiritus* in a way which does not entirely correspond to the insights of the Reformation but which, far from contradicting it, rather enriches it. Let us add that, thus, she is *creatura Verbi et Spiritus* in the way in which Christ, her head, is held by the Son and the Spirit as soon as he comes into this world ("in Jesus Christ, his only *Son* . . . who was begotten by the Holy *Spirit*) during his ministry ("Jesus with the power of the Spirit taught in their synagogues" [Luke 4:15, cf. 4:1, 18–19]) at his resurrection and in his dominical acts.[5]

Inserting the Church at the intersection of the three levels of grace makes it possible, right from the beginning, to set the horizon for the three great perceptions which have guided the life of the Church of God from her very beginning, both as a whole and for each of her members. First of all, as the apostolic texts state, she is a community of the "poor" (in the very rich sense of the terms used for poverty in Scripture) for whom the law of brotherly aid (Acts 2:44–45; 4:32–36) and of solidarity with all those who are excluded, infirm, despised, and miserable are infinitely more than philanthropic duties foreign to her real nature. They are, on the contrary, inseparable from her being *en Christô*. Her place is where grace enters into human distress, supremely revealed in the cross.

On the other hand, the Church of God always holds within herself the Spirit's call to *metanoia*. This conversion does not only mean snatching her members from the claws of the powers of evil but also constantly readjusting to the ways which God chooses to work out his plan. There are perversions of collective desire whose consequences are far worse than those of individuals.

But above all, the Church of God knows that she is shaped by "the two hands of God" into a *communion (koinônia)* which means, inseparably, the participation in the communion of the Trinitarian life and the solidarity with the brotherhood of the body of Christ. There is for her the essence which explains all the rest, which derives from and depends upon it.

It seems to us that building on the achievements of the last thirty years, we can, all together and irrespective of our denomination, come to a consensus of very great importance. Because, by this agreement, if we all consent to place the Church of God at the intersection of the three basic levels of grace, we manifest our unanimity about what is essential and what scholasticism calls the *res Ecclesiae*. This agreement is more radical than the basis of the World Council of Churches. In fact, it is on a quite different level since it immediately concerns our being *before God*.

We will then discover how our alliances in the *diakonia* for humankind in distress are acts of the Church, contracted by all in a unity which can be very deep in this undertaking. They are not foreign to our common belonging to the world of grace; they derive from it.

We also note that the *aggiornamento* of our ways of living the Gospel—and enterprises as demanding as the one to which the Lima document (BEM) calls us—first of all aim to lead us, or lead us back, to authenticity. These are acts of the *gratia veritatis,* in the biblical sense. Whatever one may think of it, the Reformation, for instance, primarily wanted to be one of those acts. Therefore, despite the resistance or irritation which they can provoke, the conclusions of the bilateral dialogues and of the Faith and Order studies can actually help to reevaluate, confirm, make "receivable," or even go beyond these desires for metanoia which have become occasions for division and not for the conversion of the whole. The intuition of the Truth which they have, and which the confessions they produced wanted to keep, must be made "appropriate" by all. But, correlatively, when the dialogues which we have mentioned ask the confessions of all traditions to revise their doctrines and their way of acting at central points, it is still a question of the same kind of conversion, aiming at full harmony with the *gratia Veritatis* by which the Church of God finds herself encompassed. It is therefore not a question of subordinating this call to conversion to confessional loyalty but, on the contrary, to subject this loyalty to the imperatives of the metanoia. These imperatives have not been encapsulated in the institutions of the Reformation, nor identified with it. The *gratia* continues to heal and to restore in all the churches the desire for authenticity which has been so often obscured by the dreams of *hybris.* Each church is grasped in the *dunamis* of the Spirit of Truth.

But this only becomes real on the fundamental level of the *koinōnia.* In the constitution *Lumen Gentium* and in the decree *Unitatis Redintegratio,* the Catholic Church recognizes that beyond its canonical frontiers there exist more than *vestigia Ecclesiae,* there are *elementa Ecclesiae*—realities of grace which make the Church—and thus she opens up an ecclesiological perspective which can be valid for all Christian communities. The extent of the field of action of the Spirit of God does not correspond to the canonical limits of the churches, even of the oldest ones. There is Church outside the churches.[6] This perspective allows the "recognition" of a true but imperfect communion between all the Churches. We have described it as "the communion of the Church of God inseparably intra et extra." But it is crucial to stress that in this *koinōnia* which overflows the canonical frontiers, it is the communion with God, instituted by the Word and the Spirit (his "two hands") and based on his own *hesed-we-emeth* (mercy and faithfulness), which constitutes the basic link human divisions cannot break.

We need to change our usual outlook. Instead of concentrating on human faithlessness, we have to look to God's faithfulness. Certainly, faithlessness is the object of the metanoia which we mentioned earlier, and no Christian community can avoid the call to conversion as we have defined it. Nevertheless, to use a formula of St. Augustine for the common experience, the call can be summed up thus: "Become what you are," convert yourselves to the *koinōnia* with which I have sealed you, let me shape you with my "two hands" into perfect and full *koinōnia*.

Therefore we ask: what will an ecumenical ecclesiology, built on this Trinitarian basis of grace, consist of? Based on the work of the Word and the Spirit, it will bring together all those elements of the common *diakonia*, of the common metanoia, and of the true but imperfect communion. Thus one can discover how, on the basis of the Father's faithfulness which is always on offer, the Church of God must understand and structure herself to be truly, fully, and visibly "humankind restored under grace." It is in the very life of the churches and not in some totally abstract speculation, that one has to look for the materials for this study of the true face of the Church. And it is in her relations with humankind *as such*, in the diversity of situations and cultures, that God's plan has to be more deeply understood.

Therefore we do not seek an inventive or prospective ecclesiology, much less a deductive one, but, on the contrary, an ecclesiology which discovers on the faces of the different "confessions" the features inscribed there by God's faithfulness and, from there, fathoms the nature of the Church of God. According to the letter to the Ephesians properly understood, was not the Church given with Christ's resurrection?

The forces of evil can shake her as much as they want and lead to the scandalous wound of schism, but they can never erase from the Church, "un-do" (*indefectibilitas*) the mark of God's faithfulness.

Certainly, the Church is present in the world in very different states. Sometimes her essential features are hidden under sediments which obscure them. Sometimes they are disfigured by excrescences which unbalance the work of the Spirit. Sometimes she is weak in the essential means of grace which God wills her to have. Sometimes they are all present but without their proper brilliance. In any case, even if one is convinced that one's own Church of God "subsists" with everything her nature requires, there remains the sad fact that the community does not bring together all those who are "faithful to Christ." She is not *the whole* People of God. All the same, on the checkered field of these different situations and these confessional families, the real, albeit imperfect, communion comes about, as we have shown, and is held together by its relation to the Word and the Spirit. There can only be an ecumenical ecclesiology when this reality is taken seriously, holding on to all the gifts of God's grace, even where the ecclesial tissue is obviously diseased and bruised.

In particular, after the last decades of dialogue and of the statement of Vatican II—of incalculable consequences—on the "*subsistit in,*" one can no longer disregard the Christian "confessions—not in order to eliminate them but to get them to cross-fertilize, to enrich each other, correct each other, and meld into the *id quod est necessarium et sufficit.* Need we repeat that this obviously applies to the Catholic and Orthodox churches just as much as to the churches of the Reformation? It has, in fact, been the confessions (under this generic term we group together what the Lima document generally calls *churches* that have maintained the essential affirmation of faith in the express desire to be in complete harmony with the Word which reveals God's plan.[7]

One will certainly observe here that *all* the "Confessions" have not maintained *everything,* and that often *all* has not been preserved *adequately.* No doubt a Lutheran would affirm that the Catholic Church has not adequately retained the relation between justification and faith. A Catholic will say that the Anglican churches have not adequately kept the hierarchic structure of the Church by refusing to find a place for the papacy in it. An Orthodox will affirm that the churches of the West have not adequately kept the balance of the Trinitarian faith. But it is precisely in the mutual challenges between these accents or those refusals, all based on a sincere desire for Gospel authenticity, that the common search for the *id quod requiritur quia necessarium est et sufficit* must happen.

For we all know—and that is one of the other major achievements of these years of ecumenism—that there is no ecclesiology which could be directly deduced from the *Scriptura Sola,* by-passing tradition. However, as a consequence of the dramas of history, the great Tradition (which, in osmosis with Scripture, is the norm) can only be fully perceived and understood if one ignores the traditions which the "Confessions" represent. Many tributaries flow into the one great stream. Catholic theory has always accepted this for the Eastern traditions after the schism. Since the *"subsistit in"* of *Lumen Gentium* we have to widen the field in order to include the whole field of action of the Word and the Spirit.

May we be allowed to add—after some recent shattering experiences—that, on their side, in terms of an ecumenical ecclesiology, the churches of the Reformation must no longer exclude the Catholic tradition from what they understand to be the will of God. To say that it is "necessarily flawed and suspect" (*sic*) because of a call to study the primacy from Rome not only shows the most blatant sectarianism but also means a renunciation of the ecumenical enterprise. Anyhow, why should *hybris* only exist on the banks of the Tiber? The Evil one has many tricks . . .

The sacramental nature of the Church has to be seen against this background of grace. When she accepts the Word (faith) and the baptism in the Spirit which seals it, she is seized by "God's two hands." The full and perfect *koinônia is accomplished in the Eucharist (word and epiclesis)*, the Church as *gratia Dei* is the object of the sacramental economy. Scholasticism used to say that she is the *res Baptismi* and the *res Eucharistiae.* Because she is thus sacramentally rooted, she transcends anything juridical and belongs from the start in the realm of the charisma which shapes her reality and determines her nature.

Through this appurtenance, fruit of the sacrament, her social being itself and her activities gain their authentic Gospel color. What would otherwise be simply an organization becomes communion; what would be propaganda or expansion strategy becomes mission; what would be a theist cult becomes memorial. The Church of God is shaped in a communion of life, in the praise of God and in mission. She is only "*so-*

cietas" before God and *for the world.* These are the two coordinates of her being *en Christô,* and only by remaining at their intersection as community can she truly be Church of God, *pars humanitatis,* letting herself be seized by "God's two hands," *creatura Verbi et Spiritus* taken up in the dynamism of the *mysterion* (Eph. 1:9, 3:3–10; Rom. 16:25–26; cf. 1 Cor. 2:7–9), this plan in which she has no initiative, which is beyond her, but through which God nevertheless associates with her as his collaborator, in *communion* with himself.

It seems to us that, with a few nuances, we could manage to agree about what has been said so far. To do this, we would have to find a kind of consensus. This would be a crucial stage on our way to a full and visible communion, and also a precious theological base for our future studies. In fact, by insisting on the fact that the Church of God in its essence derives from the realms of grace, one refuses to see the institution as an absolute which dominates and governs the *oikovoμia* of salvation. But that does not mean under-estimating the importance of the institution. For there is nothing to stop it, once it is under grace, becoming one of the *elementa* without which the Church of God has not got her full identity, the full authenticity of her being *"before God"* and *"for the world."*

II. The Institution in the Power of Grace.

It is clear that in ecclesiological discussions the theme of "institution" remains one of the most thorny ones. Incidentally, if some hesitate to "receive" the Lima document (BEM), it is largely because of the section on the ministry. Recent consultations, on a level pretending to be theological, have shown that, as soon as one starts to discuss this subject, the old resistances come alive again. And the temptation revives, superficially to oppose "institution" to a free working of the Spirit. For instance, there is resistance to the statement that the institution can give ample room to charisma.

In a full ecclesiology of communion, the institution is one of the specific features of the Church of God during its stage of pilgrimage. This cannot be basically explained by the fact that, like any group which wants to live peaceably, the Church needs an organization appropriate to its aims. The need and the reason for being a properly ecclesial institution come from the fact that the group in question is a *koinōnia,* inscribed upon the tissue of history and not a simple coexistence of men and women who are organizing themselves as best they can. That is why, according to the patristic ecclesiology of communion, through the sacrament of episcopy which gives her an hierarchic authority with the necessary *exousia* to fulfill her functions, the ecclesial institution grafts itself onto the sacramental organism. She is its fruit, and that is true even back to the first origins of the power of jurisdiction. She derives from the Spirit, not from some social contract or from some decision of purely human convenience.

Let us make a very clear distinction between the ecclesial institution *as such* and institutions in the usual sense of the word. The first and radically irreplaceable role of the institution *as such* is entirely dependent on the nature of the ministry. For the traditions of the first centuries, each bishop is ordained in the apostolic continuity (or succession) and in episcopal solidarity, expressed by the laying-on of hands by bishops of other local churches who ordain him. Continuity with the origins and solidarity with the local churches *hic et nunc* means that the Eucharist at which this bishop presides and his preaching are neither those of a group parallel to the great Church which has arisen out of community in Jerusalem assembled in the fire of the Spirit at Pentecost, nor of a fraction or a sect cut off from the *koinōnia* of all the Churches of this apostolic line, *hic et nunc.* Thus, in every place, the Church manifests both her communion with the Apostles, and, through them, with Jesus Christ, who sends them, and the communion of all her communities in the same faith and the same Eucharist. God's plan to assemble humankind in solidarity, peace, justice, and reconciliation—sources of the true happiness which human desire seeks—thus emerges, "visibly" from the depth of distress of the torn world. Certainly, the expression "the humankind which God wants" bears the marks of the weakness of the Christians. The imperfection and the limits of the communion with other communities of baptized make this dramatically clear. Nevertheless, because of its sacramental origins, the episcopate which gives to the pilgrim Church of God her social structure and organizes her into a community only does so by shaping her in communion, a communion which finds its full expression in the words of the Eucharist. That is why we have to affirm that, from this point of view, the institution is one of the *elementa* which make up the authentic face of the pilgrim Church of God.

All confessions have an *episcopè,* but not all have what corresponds to what the tradition of the first centuries calls *bishops.* Between what we remember of the sacramental bishops' ordination in apostolic continuity and collegial solidarity and the way the ministry is understood in many churches, there is a more or less wide margin. Whole confessional families reject the, albeit differentiated, conclusions of BEM on a personal episcopate in line with the *episkopos* of Ignatius of Antioch.

From the point of view of an "ecumenical ecclesiology" which corresponds to an ecclesiology of communion, the problem is to discover whether and how this vision of a collective ministry—be it "non-episcopal" (*sic*), presbyterian," "multi-headed" (*sic*), "anti-monarchic" (all expressions found in the reports of recent discussions) corresponds to what we have shown to be the necessary link (in our eyes the sacramental one) which binds all the church communities with the Pentecostal apostolic community and with each other, so that they constitute one of the *elementa* or specific features of the pilgrim Church of God. Does the diversion between this vision and that of the great Tradition—reaffirmed vigorously in the Episcopal/Anglican Chicago-Lambeth Quadrilateral, and about to be adopted by Disciples of Christ—still allow us to speak about a "tolerable difference" which is compatible with the reconstitution of an authentic visible communion, or have we here a difference which is incompatible with full communion?

Discussions around this subject are not straightforward. Old demons wake up. Confessional instinct rises up against ecumenical reason or, inversely, the dream of uniformity stifles the foundations of a healthy diversity. The churches of the old episcopal tradition begin to ask themselves whether, on this point, they could not soften their demands, or "lower the bar," as one of their theologians puts it. The discussions becomes circular.

It seems to us that an "ecumenical ecclesiology" which is built on the foundations explained above and is convinced that the Church stretches beyond confessional boundaries (*Ecclesia intra et extra*) has to take account of at least two points.

If—as there is no doubt any more—the Church also extends to the non-episcopal communities, the ministry of these is included in this extension. Even if there is no formal significant act by the community to institute this ministry, such as the patristic and liturgical tradition of the early centuries demands (on the level of *signum*), it is nevertheless an instrument of the Spirit for the *communicatio* of the good things of the *communio*, which are baptism, Holy Communion (with the content one recognizes it to have), and mission. It is therefore not outside the *koinônia* which, as we have said, constitutes the axis of the ecclesial communion as such. The real if imperfect communion on which we are based is greatly indebted to it. If it falls short of being a *signum* of the visible *communio* in grace, it nevertheless is an *instrument* of its *communicatio*. We are convinced, in the light of a rather long experience of discussions in this field, that it often needs very little for such an ecclesial ministry also to become *signum*. One of the conditions for this would be that these non-episcopal confessions distance themselves, by purifying their memory, from an instinctive reaction to what appears to them to be the *hybris* of the churches of the old traditions, and that they let these explain themselves calmly. Unfortunately, experience shows how hard this task remains, even after decades of ecumenism.

One can now understand—and the history of the dialogue between the Disciples of Christ and the Catholic church is ample proof—that what is required is by no means a simple surrender, or a humiliating submission to arrogant pretensions. Instead, it means placing the ministries which are already at work in those churches into the whole, a much wider frame-work where they can find their full significance; and this while respecting a healthy diversity.

The other point we want to mention concerns the structure of episcopal ordination. It is by the sacramental act of at least three (exceptionally, two) bishops of local churches that a bishop "receives" his ministry and "is received" into this ministry, in the middle of the Eucharist of the People of God. "Continuity" in the ministry with those who followed each other on the *sedes* and "solidarity" with those who preside *hic et nunc* on other *sedes,* vertical communion through the centuries and horizontal communion which encompasses the present are radically indivisible. "Continuity" with what was transmissible in the apostolic ministry and "solidarity" with the other members of the *collegium*, relation with the origin and relation with the *hic et nunc* are equally essential. One can guess that much more is at stake here than simply validity. However a question arises now which we cannot discuss here: how can a restoration of the "solidarity" affect the *sanatio* of a defective or impaired "continuity." This question would have to be discussed not on the juridical level but on the level of the real but imperfect communion. In order to do this it would be necessary to understand if and how, in their diversity, the episcopal ministries and the other ministries which, on the level of the *signum* are separate or even opposed to each other, are on the level of instrumentality fused into the very fibre of the binding tissue of what we call "the Church overflowing its boundaries," the Church of the real if imperfect communion. For although the *signum* may be obscured by human divisions, the power of the Spirit who, on either side of the walls of separation uses these ministries as instruments of grace, keeps them united in a service which is certainly grafted upon the apostolic mandate.

It is clear that in the restored, visible *koinōnia* the question of the exercise of authority become crucial. The golden rule is to distinguish carefully between maintaining the unity *within* each of the churches involved, and maintaining the unity *between* these churches (*of* these churches with each other?). It will be a re-soldering of what are now parallel confessions which will be brought to a full *koinōnia*.

In the first case—once the stage we have described has been passed—a diversity of institutions and of "confessional" traditions which concern the behavior of communities has nothing contradictory in it, on condition that it be "visible" that, in each place, there exists only one Church: the local Church, the Church of God in full communion. It is a bit like when, today in a local Catholic Church, traditions of government as different as the Ignatian tradition, the Dominican tradition, and the Benedictine tradition live together in visible communion. Despite its tensions, the Anglican comprehensiveness can also be mentioned here. The structuring of the full and visible communion is in no way a leveling, or a disappearance of confessional riches. Some of the Church union projects in the making at present have much to teach us here, as do the failures of other unions.

More complex is the case of the ministry when it comes to the unity between the churches. Understandably we do not have time to more than touch upon the problem. However, the subject of this paper compels us to mention at least some of the principles which, elsewhere, we have explained at greater length.

In the perspective of an "ecumenical ecclesiology" which, as we have said, takes the "confessional factor" seriously, it is clear that such a ministry could never replace what the confessions call synodical government, conciliarity, or co-responsibility. It would be impossible to think of what the last century described as the "monarchic" exercise of authority. Equally impossible would be simply to return to the situation of the first millennium.[8] Because—always provided our parallel confessions are re-soldered together—account must be taken of the specific features certain "confessions" in the West have acquired, which are reconcilable with the full *communion* and which cannot be eradicated by a canonical decision. Everything seems to indicate that the Holy Spirit was no stranger to the appearance of these features. There is an immense difference between the meaning of the Patriarchate of the West at the time when the "crown of Patriarchs" represented the church, and the present state of the Christian West. The West is splintered. However, several of these "confessional" churches have a solid structure and an ecclesiological vision which are far from negligible. It is no accident that certain Eastern Orthodox churches are in direct dialogue with some of them, parallel to the dialogue with the Roman Catholic Church. It is possible that, between Eastern Orthodox and Romans, the ideal would be to go back, to the centuries before the break. But that is not at all true for the whole of the ecclesial world. And all the more so since, very often, the perspective is obscured. It is one thing to propose a vision of *exousia* and of the function of the magisterium as healthy as they were in the early centuries; it is quite another to dream of the concrete exercising of a primacy which would be the exact copy of the first centuries. For, whatever the vision, its implementation will always have to adapt to the context. That was already true before 1054.

For a complete survey, it would have been necessary to deal with other aspects of the title which we were given: "Towards an ecumenical ecclesiology of communion." For lack of time, we have had to leave them out. In particular, it would have been enlightening to discuss the difficult problem of what we like to call the tension between faith in Jesus Christ alone, "transcending the Church," and trust in Jesus Christ "indwelling the Church by His Spirit." The more we reflect on the (Augustinian) theme of the head/body relation, the more central this problem seems to become. But this would have led too far. We have chosen only to speak about what is germinating at present, trying to point up some ways out where, perhaps, one might be inclined to flounder in sterile pessimism. Perhaps we can at least nourish hope, and help to put in place an ecclesiology which, no longer wedded to the institution, first looks to the work of grace.

Translated by Donata Coleman

Notes

1. See *Baptism, Eucharist and Ministry, 1982–1990: Report on the Process and Responses*. Faith and Order Papers, 149 (Geneva, 1990).

2. In Michael Kinnamon, ed., *Signs of the Spirit: Official Report Seventh Assembly* (Geneva, 1991), 172–74. Also Thomas F. Best and Günther Gassmann, eds., *On the Way to Fuller Koinōnia: Official Report of the Fifth World Conference on Faith and Order*, Faith and Order Papers, 166 (Geneva, 1994), 269–70.

3. See my contribution to the Assembly of Faith and Order at Moshi, "From BEM to *Koinōnia*," *Irenikon* 69 (1996), 325–31.

4. Thus for the Concordat of Agreement between the Episcopal Church (USA) and the Evangelical Lutheran Church, see W. A. Norgren and W. G. Rusch, eds., *Toward Full Communion and "Concordat of Agreement"* Lutheran-Episcopal Dialogue Series III (Minneapolis, 1991). ECUSA is asked to renounce, for a certain time, that all of its Eucharistic ministers be ordained by a bishop (§5).

5. See our study "L'Esprit Saint et la présence de Christ dans l'Eglise, selon l'ecclésiologie de communion," to be published in *Actes du Congrès de Valence 1997*, where we quote the treatise of Didymus the Blind, *On the Trinity*: "he has given them the power to become children of God, that means of the Holy Spirit . . . he has disclosed to them that the God who begets is the Holy Spirit . . . the Spirit of God baptizes into himself and makes our body and our spirit to be reborn inseparably."

6. Compare with *Mystici Corporis* of Pius XII (1943), so rich in ecclesiological intuitions: "It is a dangerous error to affirm that one can adhere to Christ, head of the Church, without loyal submission to His vicar on earth" (§39). Cf. also *Humani Generis* (1950): "It is a doctrine based on the revealed truth, that the mystical body of Christ and the Catholic Church in communion with Rome are one and the same thing (#17).

7. One realizes this when reading the beautiful book of Carl Braaten, *La théologie luthérienne,* with commentary by Jacques Fisher (Paris, 1996).

8. This had originally been the idea of Abbot Prince Max of Saxony, in his famous article "Thoughts on the question of the union of the Churches," *Roma e l'Oriente* (November 1910) vigorously condemned by Pius X in the apostolic letter *Ex Quo,* January 3, 1911: "a hybrid unity project according to which the two Churches will in future only recognize as legitimate what was their common inheritance before the schism." One can find the letter of Pius X in Marcel Launay, *La papauté à l'aube du XXe siècle* (Paris, 1997), 297–300.

TEN

The Reception Process:
The Challenge at the Threshold
of a New Phase of the
Ecumenical Movement

Hermann J. Pottmeyer

∞

"*Koinonia/communio*" and "dialogue and reception": these are the key terms on which theologians today focus their thinking about the ongoing ecumenical process. *Koinonia/communio* describes the form of Christian unity; "dialogue and reception" describes the way to unity.

The two themes are closely connected. The way must correspond to the goal. If the goal is a *communio* of sister churches, then the way to that goal must be the beginning of a kind of behavior proper to sister churches. In the early church, which thought of itself as a *communio* of sister churches, the vital bonds between these churches were manifested in mutual exchanges or, in other words, in dialogue with one another and in the reception of traditions or confessions of faith, which each then made its own. Dialogue and reception are processes that today are already binding the separated churches together. But just as the *communio* of these churches is not yet complete, so too dialogue and reception between them is not yet complete. Therefore the effort to achieve a more complete reception of one another in Christ through dialogue in truth with one another is precisely the way that will lead to a full *communio* among sister churches.

Yesterday, Jean-Marie Tillard reflected on *communio* as the form of Christian unity; my paper will say something about reception through dialogue as the way to *communio*.

1. Reception as an Ecumenical Problem

In 1996, Cardinal Cassidy described "the question of reception" as "one of the greatest challenges facing us today."[1] In the same periodical, Konrad Raiser expressed his agreement with the cardinal. In addition to the lack of coordination among the bilateral and multilateral dialogues and to the problem of achieving, within the churches, a binding reception of the results of dialogue, Raiser mentions one reason in particular that makes this reception of the results of dialogue difficult: "The paths thus far travelled in the ecumenical movement have taken the separated churches as their starting point and sought to overcome the division by convergence and formal agreement."[2] When, in the process, many of the reasons for separation were discovered to be based on misunderstandings or to be historically conditioned and therefore no longer a reason for the separation of churches, there was already a considerable step forward.

On the other hand, each church still evaluates declarations of convergence in light of the present state of its own teaching, without checking to see whether the other traditions may not also represent a challenge to expand, complement, enrich, or even revise its own tradition: "As long as the individual churches evaluate declarations of convergence in light of the official state of their teaching, the process of reception will never advance."[3] These churches remain in the "phase of defensive protection of their own identity, which is understood as what distinguishes them from other churches."[4] What is said of declarations of convergence can be said also of the results of multilateral dialogues. These too "come up against limits in the capacity for reception, since there is no binding framework within which reception can take place."[5]

Raiser therefore suggests that we no longer regard bilateral and multilateral dialogues as simple contacts between separated churches. Rather these dialogues and their reception should be viewed as phases in a comprehensive conciliar process. His suggestion takes "for its starting point the decisive presupposition that without any action on their part, there already exists between the churches a real community that pushes them toward full catholicity. The dialogues between the churches are dialogues within community and not simply means of achieving community."[6]

Thus, the analysis of the present state of ecumenism shows (1) that the lack of reception by the churches of the past and future results of dialogue is today the most important obstacle on the road to Christian unity. (2) We are on the threshold of a new phase of ecumenism because this obstacle can be removed only by a change in the present attitude and outlook. Raiser refers to the most recent study document of the Dombes Group, which speaks of a needed "conversion" of the churches, that is, a shift of attention from what still separates them to the task of strengthening all that already binds them together and that strengthens and expands the community between them.[7]

Before going on to speak of the convergence that exists on this point between the present General Secretary of the World Council of Churches and the encyclical *Ut Unum Sint*, I must first show that the suggestion about dialogue and reception, as phases of a conciliar process, has not come out of the blue. It springs from theological reflection on what reception has meant in the ecclesial tradition and what it can mean today in the context of ecumenism.

2. Reception in the Early Church and in Present-day Ecumenism

A closer reflection on reception as an important occurrence in the life of the Church began with the Second Vatican Council, both within the Roman Catholic Church and in the ecumenical movement. In the Catholic Church, it was, first of all, the convocation of the Council and the Council itself that turned attention once more to the early church councils, the reception of which was part of the conciliar process. A second factor was the form of the early church as a *communio ecclesiarum* in which the particular Churches had their own role in the reception process. This was the idea that governed the council's reform of the church.

Both of these factors also awakened a new interest in reception within the ecumenical movement. Two further factors strengthened this interest. First, the council raised the question for the other churches and the ecumenical movement of whether and what they could receive from the council. Second, the increasing participation of Orthodox churches in the World Council of Churches from 1961 on highlighted the *communio ecclesiarum* idea of the early church, since this remained more a living reality in the eastern consciousness than in the West.[8]

After the council, this newly awakened interest in reception has led to a series of historical and systematic studies in both Catholic[9] and ecumenical theology.[10] For the time being, the climax of these studies, at the level of conferences, was reached in the ecumenical realm, at the Sixth Forum on Bilateral Dialogues in 1994[11] and, in the Catholic realm, at the Third International Colloquy of Salamanca in 1996.[12]

It can be said, speaking quite generally, that theological reflection on reception has focused on three points. A first has been historical study of the phenomenon of reception, with regard especially to the reception of conciliar decrees in the course of church history.[13] Scholars discovered how essential a role reception played in the life of the early church. A second key issue has been a more accurate conceptual and systematic definition of reception and its role in the life of the church.[14] A third has been the historical and systematic investigation of the relationship between the part played by reception and the contemporary ecclesiology in a given period. It was found that reception had its place in an ecclesiology that understood the Church to be a *koinonia*, a sacramental *communio ecclesiarum*. In a conception of the Church as a centrally governed organization or in one in which the separated churches were seen as simply a loose association with only a few bonds of community, reception did not have a theological role in its own right.

It is obvious how important all this new information is for the reform of the Catholic Church and for the ecumenical movement. It is also this new knowledge that has led to the suggestion that the reception of ecumenical dialogues should be regarded as part of a conciliar process.

For a more precise definition of reception in the early church, we can be satisfied here with Yves Congar's now classic formulation: "By 'reception' I understand here the process by which an ecclesial body truly makes its own a resolution which it had not given to itself, recognizing in the measure so promulgated a rule which is applicable to its own life."[15]

The definition contains five key elements. (1) Reception is a more or less lengthy process. (2) Reception involves an active assent that signifies an independent judgment of the recipient and is not simply an act of obedience to a higher authority. (3) The recipients—whether a particular church or a synod or a council—act as relatively independent subjects. (4) The material that is received originates, at least to a certain extent, in a source outside the recipient's own body. (5) The criterion for reception is the knowledge and experience that this material does not contradict the recipient's own tradition and shows that it will advance and enrich the inner life of the community.

In his contribution to the Third International Colloquy in Salamanca, William Henn shows that a new phase in the ecumenical discussion on reception began in the 1970s.[16] During those years the first results of ecumenical dialogue made their appearance, and the question arose of their reception by the churches. A further stimulus to this discussion came from the decision of the Faith and Order Commission in 1982 to send the Lima Document on Baptism, Eucharist, and Ministry to the churches with a request that they take an official position on it. In the course of this discussion, it was gradually realized that the classical understanding of the reception of councils could not be applied without modification to the reception of modern ecumenical texts. In 1986 Thomas Rausch described the difference as follows:

> While the classical concept emerged in a church which understood itself as a communion of churches, it was nonetheless a united

Church. In the ecumenical context, however, a new element appears; for now what is involved is a process of reception between churches separated from one another by differences of history, doctrine and structure. In the absence of communion between the churches, the process of reception is complicated considerably; as Anton Houtepen observes, "more theological consensus is needed to restore unity than to preserve unity."[17]

Despite the undeniable difference between classical reception and present-day reception of ecumenical texts, we today can still learn from the classical model. A number of renowned ecumenical theologians have developed a perspective on ecumenical reception in which they have done precisely that.[18] They suggest that we consider the reception of ecumenical documents as only one element in a broader ecumenical reception. The very fact of entering into dialogue, even prior to the production of any documents, is already an act of mutual reception that recognizes the other community as a sister to one's own community or, at least, as a partner in dialogue on the basis of an already existing communion, a partner with whom one should enter into full communion. Thus, elements of mutual reception, especially the mutual reception of the parties involved, precede the holding of a dialogue and are woven into the text which emerges from the dialogue process. Furthermore, dialogue is essentially incomplete without the reception of its results. The text, then, is only "the tip of the iceberg," as Günther Gassmann has put it.[19]

This comprehensive approach has recently gained acceptance in several ecumenical documents dealing with reception. As the Sixth Forum on Bilateral Dialogues noted:

> Ecumenical reception is the comprehensive process by which the churches make their own the whole range of results of their encounters with each other. It is thus far more than the official response to the results of dialogues, although such responses are essential. Reception is an integral part of the movement toward . . . full communion.[20]

A further element in this new conception of reception, and an inheritance from the classical model of reception, is that it understands the agents of this comprehensive process to include all of the members of the Church, while specifying the particular roles of church leaders, of the whole body of the faithful, and of theologians. As Cardinal Willebrands said:

> Inasmuch as the entire people of God partakes in the search for and the unfolding of the truth of God's word, all the charisms and services are involved according to their station: the theologians by means of their research activities, the faithful by means of their preserving fidelity and piety, the ecclesial ministries and especially the college of bishops with its function of making binding doctrinal decisions. One can say that ministry and charism, proclamation and theology, magisterial ministry and sense of faith of the people, all act together in the reception process.[21]

The same three agents of reception are to be found in one of the reports of the Sixth Forum on Bilateral Dialogues where it states: "Within the process of reception, church leaders, theologians and the people as a whole each have a part to play in accordance with their various responsibilities."[22] The Directory of the Pontifical Council for Promoting Christian Unity (1993) likewise speaks, emphatically and in detail, of the participation of all members of the Church in the reception process and of the triad of agents of reception. It does so in paragraphs 179–82, which are devoted entirely to the subject of reception.[23] That same Directory also speaks of the spiritual climate in which alone there can be a successful ecumenical reception: "The life of faith and the prayer of faith, no less than reflection on the doctrine of faith, enter into this process of Reception, by which the whole Church, under the inspiration of the Holy Spirit . . . makes her own the fruits of a dialogue, in a process of listening, of testing, of judging and of living."[24]

The necessity of conversion for a successful reception is made very clear in the report of the Sixth Forum on Bilateral Dialogues:

> The movement of the churches towards fuller communion with each other is only possible when they are open to renewal. Mutual openness, the removal of dividing differences of faith and order,

and the reconciliation of memories presuppose changes of perspective and attitude. Without such a process of spiritual renewal, no progress towards visible unity is possible.

Consequently, reception of the results of ecumenical dialogues on the way towards unity both presupposes and furthers such renewal. Without a readiness to be renewed by the experiences and insights of other traditions, a church and its members are not inclined to receive the results of a dialogue. Dialogue exposes a church to the challenges and enriching gifts it may receive from other traditions. Reception and renewal are thus two aspects of the same reality of moving towards fuller communion.[25]

This spiritual ecumenism is undoubtedly a decisive element in the comprehensive conception of reception and the soul of the mutual reception of one another that precedes and accompanies the reception of the documents.

3. The Contribution of the Encyclical *Ut Unum Sint*

As a third step I want to take a brief look at the encyclical *Ut Unum Sint* (1995) insofar as it deals with our subject. After the decree *Unitatis Redintegratio* of the Second Vatican Council, this encyclical is undoubtedly the most important official statement issued by the Roman Catholic Church on the subject of ecumenism. The encyclical surprised many with its excellence, its strong backing of ecumenical concern and progress, and its forward-looking attitude. On essential points, of course, it follows *Unitatis Redintegratio,* but there are some new emphases. The question I am asking is this: Is there a convergence here with the proposal of Konrad Raiser, which I sketched in my first step and the development of which I traced in my second?

Let us look first at the understanding of dialogue and reception. In its first chapter the encyclical offers a remarkable anthropology of dialogue.[26] From this it derives the criterion of "reciprocity." It then makes this important observation:

It is necessary to pass from antagonism and conflict to a situation where each party recognizes the other as a partner. When undertaking dialogue, each side must presuppose in the other a desire for reconciliation, for unity in truth. For this to happen, any display of mutual opposition must disappear. Only thus will dialogue help to overcome division and lead us closer to unity. (§29)

This requirement corresponds exactly to Raiser's proposal that others be perceived and accepted not as separated churches but as partners and eventually as sister churches. The issue, then, is the mutual reception of one another that precedes and accompanies the reception of the results of dialogue, and, therefore, the comprehensive conception of reception.

The encyclical describes spiritual ecumenism as the "soul" of the new outlook (§28). Spiritual ecumenism plays a very important role in the encyclical, which speaks at length of the "primacy of prayer" (§21–30) and of "renewal and conversion" (§15–17). Conversion helps to change the "way of looking at things"; it causes other Christians and Churches to be seen in a new light and leads to the discovery of their riches of sanctity, holy men and women, and Christian commitment. At the same time, this conversion makes one aware of one's own imperfections and sins against other Christians and so opens the way to one's own renewal (§15). For this reason, the encyclical speaks repeatedly of "the dialogue of conversion" (§82).

Part of the common ground created by dialogue and reception is a shared view of the criterion for binding truth. The encyclical says, "By engaging in frank dialogue, Communities help one another to look at themselves together in the light of the Apostolic Tradition. This leads them to ask themselves whether they truly express in an adequate way all that the Holy Spirit has transmitted through the Apostles" (§16).

The encyclical is the first papal document to deal expressly with ecumenical reception and to describe this as a new challenge (§80–81). In the third chapter we read, "A new task lies before us: that of receiving the results already achieved. These cannot remain the statements of bilateral commissions but must become a common heritage" (§80).

Like the documents mentioned earlier, the encyclical, too, speaks of the triad of agents of reception (§80–81). It describes reception in greater detail as "a broad and precise critical process which analyzes the results and rigorously tests their consistency with the Tradition of faith received from the Apostles and lived out in the community of believers" (§80). This description of reception as "critical process" is entirely in keeping with the classical understanding of reception. But, as was already the case in the early church, it raises the question of the criteria of truth. It is noteworthy that here and in other passages the encyclical refers not simply to the present state of the teaching of the Catholic Church but to the Tradition of the Apostles as still taught and lived in the church today. By this tradition is undoubtedly meant, also and not least, the tradition of faith of the Catholic Church. In fact, in another passage and with a reference to *Unitatis Redintegratio*, the encyclical declares that the full truth of Christ has always been maintained in this church (§10–11). But this declaration is accompanied by distinctions.

As the encyclical says in the passage on dialogue that I cited a moment ago, the Catholic Church submits itself, along with the other churches, to the critical question of "whether they truly express in an adequate way all that the Holy Spirit has transmitted through the Apostles" (§16). This self-critical question is part of reception as a "critical process." The encyclical further declares that "certain features of the Christian mystery have at times been more effectively emphasized" in the other churches (§14). Consequently, it does not insist on the formulation of the faith that has come down to us in the Catholic Church as the sole criterion of truth. It regards it as possible that in the reception of ecumenical dialogue, the way in which the truth of the faith has thus far been expressed in its own tradition may prove less helpful on the way to unity in the truth. Thus the encyclical says:

> Taking up an idea expressed by Pope John XXIII at the opening of the Council, the Decree on Ecumenism mentions the way of formulating doctrine as one of the elements of a continuing reform. . . . [For] doctrine needs to be presented in a way that makes it understandable to those for whom God himself intends it (§18–19).

For this reason, it is said at the end of the section on reception, "In all this, it will be a great help methodologically to keep carefully in mind the distinction between the deposit of faith and the formulation in which it is expressed, as Pope John XXIII recommended in his opening address at the Second Vatican Council" (§81).

If I understand the encyclical correctly, Pope John Paul II already applies this methodology to the question of the Petrine office. He accepts "the request made of me to find a way of exercising the primacy which, while in no way renouncing what is essential to its mission, is nonetheless open to a new situation" (§95). The pope cautiously distinguishes between the modern absolutist and centralist exercise of the primacy and the biblically based Petrine office and its exercise during the first millennium, and he invites other Christians "to engage with me in a patient and fraternal dialogue on this subject, a dialogue in which, leaving useless controversies behind, we could listen to one another, keeping before us only the will of Christ for his Church and allowing ourselves to be deeply moved by his plea" for unity (§96).

As has already become clear, an integral understanding of reception depends on emphasizing no longer the separation but rather the existing common ground and community among the partners in dialogue. It is in this respect that the encyclical displays the greatest advance beyond the Decree on Ecumenism. The many ecumenical encounters of which the pope speaks in his encyclical have evidently enabled him to share the same experience.

Thus he writes that "the one Church of Christ is effectively present" in other Christian communities (§11). And again, "it is not that beyond the boundaries of the Catholic community there is an ecclesial vacuum" (§13). The encyclical describes as "a basic ecclesiological statement" the wish expressed in the Directory of the Pontifical Council for a reciprocal official recognition of baptisms (§42). In chapter two, "brotherhood rediscovered" is listed as the first of "the fruits of dialogue." The text goes on to say: "There is an increased awareness that we all belong to Christ. I have personally been able many times to observe this. . . . The 'universal brotherhood' of Christians has become a firm ecumenical conviction" (§42).

The encyclical sees one sign of this new outlook in a changed vocabulary, which it too accepts. People are speaking increasingly, not of "separated brothers," but of "other Christians" or "others who have received Baptism" or "Christians of other Communities." The Directory describes other communities as "Churches and Ecclesial Communities that are not in full communion with the Catholic Church" (§42).

The pope sees the division as having been overcome most of all in the spiritual realm. It is worth noting that in his view the very close union of Christians has already been accomplished "in the full communion of the Saints" and especially in a "common Martyrology" (§84). The pope speaks of the martyrs several times. In the introduction he says, "These brothers and sisters of ours, in the selfless offering of their lives for the Kingdom of God, are the most powerful proof that every factor of division can be transcended and overcome in the total gift of self for the sake of the Gospel" (§1). In the third chapter he writes: "I have already remarked, and with deep joy, how an imperfect but real communion is preserved and is growing. . . . I now add that this communion is already perfect in what we all consider the highest point of the life of grace, *martyria* unto death, the truest communion possible with Christ" (§89).

The pope also asks the provocative question: "Is not this same attachment at the heart of what I have called a 'dialogue of conversion'? Is it not precisely this dialogue which clearly shows the need for an ever more profound experience of the truth if full communion is to be attained?" (§83). In fact, Orthodox, Protestant, and Catholic Christians had precisely this experience in the concentration camps and gulags of our century. Rarely has this experience been acknowledged in this way in an official document.

But the encyclical sees community being established even in ecumenical dialogues. It says, "The bilateral theological dialogues carried on with the rhajor Christian Communities start from a recognition of the degree of communion already present" (§49). The striking emphasis of the encyclical on contacts with the churches of the East has attracted both attention and criticism. And yet, independently of any supposed ecumenical tactics, this emphasis follows naturally from the very starting point of the encyclical. For it is because of the more complete community in faith and order with these churches that the dialogue with them comes closest to the model of "dialogue and reception among sister Churches."

Thus an analysis of the encyclical *Ut Unum Sint* shows an extensive convergence with the proposals of the General Secretary of the World

Council of Churches as to how the challenge raised by the task of reception can be met by a more complete and rounded understanding of what reception is.

4. Remaining Disagreements and Reception

In a fourth and final step, I want to turn to the question of remaining disagreements. This question arises not only as a task of further dialogues but also, and in a special way, as a task for reception. Thus, for example, the very important Lutheran-Roman Catholic Common Statement on "Church and Justification" (1994) reaches a fundamental agreement on the question of justification; and yet a section entitled "Areas of Controversy" lists a series of remaining disagreements.[27] Similar remarks occur in other ecumenical documents. The question arises, therefore, of the reception of such documents.

It can be said, first of all, that the common acknowledgment of remaining disagreements already represents ecumenical progress. For this common acknowledgment does not detract from the existing common ground and community but, on the contrary, is an expression of it and strengthens it. This is certainly the view of the encyclical *Ut Unum Sint,* which lists five such areas (§79). In addition, the disagreements differ among themselves in importance and are not unaffected by agreements already reached. This is especially true if they are seen in the setting of a dynamic process of dialogue and reception in which others are taken seriously as partners and their concerns are regarded as possible enrichments of one's own tradition.

In dealing with remaining disagreements in the process of dialogue and reception, two kinds of criteria may be distinguished in principle. The first kind I would call critical for the differentiation and evaluation of disagreements, the second kind, criteria of truth. Three criteria for the differentiation and evaluation of remaining disagreements can be found in the encyclical *Ut Unum Sint.* The first I have already cited; it is "the distinction between the deposit of faith and the formulation in which it is expressed" (§81). If a disagreement has its basis only or chiefly in traditional formulations, then it is necessary "to find the formula which, by capturing the reality in its entirety, will enable us to move beyond partial readings and eliminate false interpretations" (§38). For "the element which determines communion in truth is the *meaning of truth*. The expression of truth can take different forms" (§91).

The encyclical gives as a second criterion, the "order or 'hierarchy' of truths, since they vary in their relationship to the foundation of the Christian faith" (§37). In fact, a joint working out of the relationship of controverted doctrines with the foundation of the Christian faith (that is, with the mystery of Christ and the coming of the reign of God) can help in grasping the differing importance of disagreements, in understanding the concerns of others, and perhaps in jointly setting new priorities that will open the way to an agreement. This point was also made in *The Notion of "Hierarchy of Truths:" An Ecumenical Interpretation*, a study document commissioned and received by the Joint Working Group of the Roman Catholic Church and the World Council of Churches in 1990.[28]

The third criterion reads: In the process "towards the necessary and sufficient visible unity . . . one must not impose any burden beyond that which is strictly necessary (see Acts 15:28)" (§18). Jean-Marie Tillard has underscored the importance of this criterion, "'Reception' is thus found to be completely dependent on the definition of the phrase *id quod requiritur et sufficit*."[29]

As a matter of fact, these three criteria make clear the possibility of a plurality of ways of expressing and living the faith, without harming or lessening the communion in truth. Such a plurality is already to be seen in the New Testament writings and in the churches of the first millennium. All three criteria for differentiating and evaluating remaining disagreements are thus an important help in showing whether or not these disagreements are an obstacle to the acceptance of full communion.

The criteria of truth are necessarily connected with the foregoing criteria, but they are the decisive ones in the final analysis. The problem that arises for reception at this point was mentioned at the beginning of my lecture. It is the inclination of churches to receive ecumenical documents solely on the basis of their own traditions. Tillard criticizes the similar outlook which accepts "from the agreed text only 'what has always been thought and stated' within its own tradition and refuses anything which challenges or is alien to it. In this case, the tradition of the group becomes the gauge of acceptance, a stand which implies the refusal to risk becoming seriously involved."[30]

As the criteria of truth according to the Roman Catholic Church, the encyclical *Ut Unum Sint* lists: "Sacred Scripture and the great Tradition of the Church. Catholics have the help of the Church's living Magisterium" (§39). Or, in the formulation cited earlier, "The tradition of faith received from the Apostles and lived out in the community of believers gathered around the Bishop, their legitimate Pastor" (§80).

In fact, however, the normative role of tradition and the magisterium is disputed among the churches. The encyclical *Ut Unum Sint* lists among the five still controversial areas: "(1) the relationship between Sacred Scripture, as the highest authority in matter of faith, and Sacred Tradition, as indispensable to the interpretation of the Word of God," and "(4) the Magisterium of the Church, entrusted to the Pope and the Bishops in communion with him, understood as a responsibility and an authority exercised in the name of Christ for teaching and safeguarding the faith" (§79).

The clarification and removal of these disagreements is an urgent task because further ecumenical reception depends on it in great measure. Unless I am completely wrong, two distinct problems, and the confusion of the two, play a role in the disagreements mentioned. A first and more basic problem is to be seen in the churches of the Reformation and has to do with the acceptance of the normative role of the church, its tradition, and its magisterium in the communication and preservation of revelation. For it was part of the original experience of these churches that the church, at times and in part, failed in this function. The other problem arises out of the hermeneutical difficulties in the interpretation of tradition and in making the necessary distinction between binding "Tradition" (with a capital *T*) and purely human "traditions." Not infrequently this second problem is assigned a more fundamental significance because it is confused with the first.

In this regard, it may be noted that the hermeneutical difficulties are no fewer in the interpretation of the Sacred Scriptures. In addition, it must be observed that all the churches which reject universal tradition as a rule of truth in the interpretation of the Scriptures and insist on their own particular tradition as sole criterion of truth, do not adopt a credible point of view. Finally, it must be said that the concrete hermeneutical difficulties arising in the interpretation of Sacred Scripture and ecclesial tradition do not in themselves form a problem specific to any tradition or one that should separate churches. This problem, after all, arises even within the Roman Catholic Church (think, for example, of the discussion among Catholics of the ordination of women) and it also arises within the other churches. Even the as yet undivided church of the first millennium faced the problem, as can be seen from Vincent of Lerins' *Commonitorium* in the fifth century. *Ut Unum Sint* refers to norms of truth developed at that time when it says that matters of faith "require universal consent, extending from the Bishops to the lay faithful, all of whom have received the anointing of the Holy Spirit. It is the same Spirit who assists the Magisterium and awakens the *senus fidei*" (§80).

What, then, is to be done? Ecumenical agreement is already being started regarding the normative role of the church—that is, of the entire people of God and the magisterium—and also regarding the fundamental distinction between "Tradition" with a capital *T* and "traditions." But further clarification is needed, and the question is closely connected with the question of justification.

With regard to the second problem, namely, an agreement on "Tradition" its hermeneutical assessment, and its binding force, it is desirable that the Tradition of the as yet undivided church of the first millennium, especially its Christological and Trinitarian doctrinal decrees and its status as a *communio ecclesiarum*, be given priority over the later confessional developments of a particular church. This is not a plea for a fossilized classicism. What is being recommended is rather the path of a patient re-reception (to use Yves Congar's term) of this great and universal Tradition and its decisions. Such a re-reception not only takes its bearings from the past, but at the same time it heeds the "signs of the times," above all the urging of the Spirit to a full community of churches and the need of a credible preaching by a reconciled Christianity.

Common statements about the profession of the Nicene-Constantinopolitan Creed, as well as many other ecumenical documents, have already been following this path. The Roman Catholic Church expressly follows it in its relation with the churches of the East. Many voices in Rome point out that Rome is striving for an ecumenical agreement on the Petrine office on the basis of the first millennium and the exercise of the primacy during that period. In *Ut Unum Sint* we read: "For a whole millennium Christians were united in a 'brotherly fraternal communion of faith and sacramental life. . . . If disagreements in belief and discipline arose among them, the Roman See acted by common consent as moderator'" (§95). In 1982 Cardinal Ratzinger was already writing, "When it comes to the doctrine of the primacy, Rome must not demand more of the East than was formulated and taught in the first millennium."[31]

The first millennium also provides a model for ecumenical reception in our day. Although it is true that "more theological consensus is needed to restore unity than to preserve unity" and that there is consequently a certain difference between classical reception and present-day ecumenical reception, Edward Kilmartin is correct in saying that "as in the case of Nicaea I, Chalcedon and the rest of the so-called ecumenical councils of the first millennium, reception took place through a more or less complicated process."[32]

I want to end with a citation from the 1985 statement of the Inter-Orthodox Symposium on the Lima documents; it takes its direction from the classical concept of reception: "Reception at this stage is a step forward in the 'process of our growing together in mutual trust . . .' towards doctrinal convergence and ultimately towards 'communion with one another in continuity with the apostles and the teachings of the universal Church.'"[33]

Notes

1. Edward I. Cardinal Cassidy, "Welche nächsten Schritte in der Ökumene sind überfällig, realisierbar und wünschenswert?," *Una Sancta* 51 (1996), 117.

2. Konrad Raiser, "Welche nächsten Schritte in der Ökumene sind überfällig, realisierbar und wünschenswert?," ibid., 123.

3. Ibid., 124.

4. Ibid., 126.

5. Ibid., 124.

6. Ibid., 123.

7. Ibid., 126; Groupe des Dombes, *Pour la conversion des Églises* (Paris, 1991).

8. See Thomas P. Rausch, "Reception Past and Present," *Theological Studies* 47 (1986), 497–508; William G. Rusch, *Reception—An Ecumenical Opportunity* (Philadelphia, 1988), 13–32; Franz Wolfinger, "Die Rezeption theologischer Einsichten und ihre theologische und ökumenische Bedeutung: von der Einsicht zur Verwirklichung," *Catholica* 31 (1977), 202–33; Hermann J. Pottmeyer, "Rezeption und Gehorsam: Aktuelle Apsekte der wiederentdeckten Realität 'Rezeption,'" in Wolfgang Beinert, ed., *Glaube als Zustimmung. Zur Interpretation kirchlicher Rezeptionsvorgänge* (Freiburg, 1991), 51–91.

9. See Aloys Grillmeier "Konzil und Rezeption: Methodische Bemerkungen zu einem Thema der ökumenischen Diskussion der Gegenwart," *Theologie und Philosophie* 45 (1970), 321–52; idem, "The Reception of Chalcedon in the Roman Catholic Church," *Ecumenical Review* 22 (1970), 383–411; Yves Congar, "La Réception comme réalité ecclésiologique," *Revue des sciences philosophiques et théologiques* 56 (1972), 369–403; Giuseppe Alberigo, Jean-Pierre Jossua, and Joseph a Komochat, eds., *The Reception of Vatican II* (Washington, D.C., 1987); Aloys Klein, "Rezeption der ökumenischen Dialoge," in Klaus Lüdicke, Heinrich Mussinghoff, and Hugo Schwendenwein, eds., *Justus Iudex* (Essen, 1990), 31–39; Wolfgang Beinert, ed., *Glaude als Zustimmung: Zur Interpretation kirchlicher Rezeptionsvorgänge* (Freiburg, 1991); Gilles Routhier, *La réception d'un concile* (Paris, 1993); Jean-Marie R. Tillard, "La réception comme exigence oecuménique," in Gillian R. Evans, and Michael Gourgues, ed., *Communion et réunion. Mélanges J.M.R. Tillard* (Louvain, 1995), 75–94; Angel Antón, "La 'recepción' en la Iglesia y eclesiologia (I)," *Gregorianum* 77 (1996), 57–96.

10. See Liviu Stan, "On the Reception of the Decisions of Ecumenical Councils by the Church," *Councils and the Ecumenical Movement,* WCC Studies 5 (Geneva, 1968), 68–75; Werner Küppers "Reception, Prolegomena to a Systematic Study," ibid., 76–98; Kurt Schmidt-Clausen "Die Rezeption ökumenischen Bewegung," *Ökumenische Rundschau* 27 (1978), 1–13; Franz Wolfinger, "Theological Reception and Ecumenism," *Theology Digest* 27 (1979), 243–48; Peter Lengsfeld, and Hermann Stobbe, eds., *Theologischer Konsens und Kirchenspaltung* (Mainz, 1981); Lukas Vischer, "The Reception of Consensus in the Ecumenical Movement," *One in Christ* 17 (1981), 294–305; Max Thurian, ed., *Ecumenical Perspectives on Baptism, Eucharist and Ministry* (Geneva, 1983), 140–60; Johannes Cardinal Willebrands, "Ecumenical Dialogue and its Reception," *One in Christ* 21 (1985), 217–25; World Council of Churches, "BEM Reception: Experiences, Reflections, Significance," in *Faith and Renewal: Stavanger 1985* (Geneva, 1986), 89–92; Jean-Marie Tillard "Fondements ecclésiologiques de la 'réception' oecuménique," *Toronto Journal of Theology* 3 (1987), 28–40; James A. Coriden, "The Reception of Ecumenical

Accords in a World Church," *Jurist* 49 (1989), 48–68; see also the contributions in *Irenikon* 58 (1985) and 59 (1986); Hermann Fischer "Rezeption in ihrer Bedeutung für Leben und Lehre der Kirche: Vorläufige Erwägungen zu einem undeutlichen Begriff," *Zeitschrift für Theologie und Kirche* 87 (1990), 100–123; Jean-Marie Tillard "Reception—Communion," *One in Christ* 28 (1992), 307–22.

11. *Reports of the Sixth Forum on Bilateral Dialogues 1994* (Geneva, 1995), 5–24.

12. III. Colloque International Salamanque 1996: *La réception et la communion entre les églises* (forthcoming).

13. See Aloys Grillmeier, "The Reception of Church Councils," in Paul McShane, ed., *Foundations of Theology* papers from the International Lonergan Congress (Dublin, 1971), 102–14; Hermann J. Sieben, *Die Konzilsidee der Alten Kirche* (Paderborn, 1979); Edward J. Kilmartin "Reception in History: An Ecclesiological Phenomenon and its Significance," *Journal of Ecumenical Studies* 21 (1984), 34–54; Klaus Schatz "Rezeption ökumenischer Konzilien im ersten Jahrtausend: Schwierigkeiten, Formen der Bewältigung und verweigerte Rezeption," in Wolfgang Beinert, ed., *Glaube als Zustimmung*, 93–122.

14. See the comprehensive bibliography in Angel Antón, "La 'receptión' en la Iglesia y eclesiología (1) and (II)"; III. Colloque International Salamanque 1996, *La réception et la communion entre les églises* (forthcoming).

15. Yves Congar, "La réception comme réalité ecclésiologique," 370.

16. William Henn, "The Reception of Ecumenical Documents," in III. Colloque International Salamanque 1996, *La réception et la communion entre les églises*.

17. Thomas P. Rausch, "Reception Past and Present," 500.

18. Günther Gassman "Rezeption im ökumenische Kontext," *Ökumenische Rundschau* 26 (1977), 314–27; idem, "Die Rezeption der Dialoge," ibid. 33 (1984), 357–68; idem, "The Official Responses to the Lima Document," *Ecumenical Trends* 15 (1986), 186–88; see also John D. Zizioulas "The Theological Problem of 'Reception,'" *One in Christ* 21 (1985), 187–93; Jean-Marie Tillard, "Reception—Communion."

19. Günther Gassmann, "Die Rezeption der Dialoge," 362.

20. *Reports of the Sixth Forum on Bilateral Dialogues 1994*, 5.

21. Johannes Cardinal Willebrands, "The Ecumenical Dialogue and its Reception," 222.

22. *Reports of the Sixth Forum on Bilateral Dialogues 1994*, 6.

23. Pontifical Council for Promoting Christian Unity, *Directory for the Applications of the Principles and Norms of Ecumenism*, paragraphs 179–82.

24. Ibid., paragraph 180.8.

25. *Reports of the Sixth Forum on Bilateral Dialogues 1994*, 7.

26. Pope John Paul II, encyclical letter *Ut Unum Sint* (25 May 1995) in *Origins* 25 (1995) 49–72. All citations in the text are to paragraphs.

27. Lutheran-Roman Catholic Statement "Church and Justification," 1994, paragraphs 174–241.

28. (Geneva, 1990), 16–24.

29. Jean-Marie Tillard, "'Reception': A Time to Beware of False Steps," in *Ecumenical Trends* 14 (1985), 148.

30. Tillard, 146.

31. Joseph Cardinal Ratzinger *Theologische Prinzipienlehre: Bausteine zur Fundamentaltheologie* (Munich, 1981) 209.

32. Edward G. Kilmartin, "Reception in History," 38.

33. Max Thurian, ed., *Churches Respond to BEM* 1 (Geneva, 1986), 124.

ELEVEN

Power and Authority in Ecumenical Theology

Stephen Sykes

∽

I am tempted, on occasions when the matter of power and authority is being discussed in ecumenical theological circles, to turn to the letter of Jude. It was written, according to the scholarly consensus, at the end of the first century, by a Jewish Christian in deep anxiety about the insinuation of false teachers into the church. Twelve out of the twenty-five verses of this short writing describe their activities in the most unflattering of terms:

They are enemies of religion; they pervert the free favour of our God into licentiousness, disowning Jesus Christ (4);

These deluded dreamers continue to defile their bodies, flout authority, and insult celestial beings (8);

They have followed the way of Cain; for profit they have plunged into Balaam's error; they have rebelled like Korah and they share his fate (11);

They are wild sea waves; foaming with disgraceful deeds; they are stars that have wandered from their courses, and the place reserved for them is an eternity of blackest darkness (13);

They are a set of grumblers and malcontents. They follow their lusts.

Bombast comes rolling from their lips, and they court favour to gain their ends (16);

These people create divisions, they are worldly and unspiritual (19).

This author, I conclude, was no Anglican. He was also a stranger to the elaborate courtesies of modern ecumenism. The enemies he denounces, we note, are already inside the church:

certain individuals have wormed their way in, the very people whom scripture long ago marked down for the sentence they are now incurring (4).

They are being threatened with divine judgment by a writer under the convention of pseudonymity, claiming to be the brother of Jesus.[1]

It is more than tempting to ignore this apparently marginal piece of the canon. Selective blindness to difficult parts of the tradition is a recurrent feature of theologies with an apologetic purpose. And, of course, ecumenism has a worthy apologetic aim, that of restoring the lost institutional unity of the Church of God. My suggestion that we do not forget the letter of Jude is an invitation to acknowledge how profoundly formative to the biblical process of institution-building was the threat of deviation from the faith, morally and doctrinally; and how extreme are the resources of rhetoric available to those who consider the unity of the faith to be at risk.

In Christian history the letter of Jude has had a variable reputation. Though it stood in the Muratorian canon and was regarded by Tertullian and Clement of Alexandria as canonical, both Eusebius of Caesarea and Jerome placed it among "disputed writings." Luther pointedly failed to enumerate it among the principal books of the New Testament; Calvin, on the other hand, considered it a timely weapon against the Anabaptists. A modern Protestant biblical critic spoke of "irreconcilable discord" between it and the understanding of faith in the main New Testament witnesses.[2] But these doubts are beside the point. Jude is irrefutable evidence from the late first century that

Christian communities found themselves shaken to the very core of their being by internal deviations from the faith, and in response acutely sharpened the boundaries between truth and falsity in order to exclude the latter. Similar evidence is available from a social-historical reading of the Gospel of John and the Johannine letters. By the time we arrive at the second-century church, when the formative conflicts with Gnosticism are at their height, these letters are among the texts deployed by orthodox critics against their opponents.[3] The whole process of the development of authoritative resources, a canon of sacred writings together with privileged interpreters of their meaning, is generated by the threat of disintegration. The very identity of the covenant people of God is at stake (we note the invocation of the memory of Cain, Balaam, and Korah). It is a theme already identified in Saint Paul's letters to the Galatians (1:6–9). About such matters there can be no compromise.

And yet even the letter of Jude shows the existence of areas of ambiguity. One further reason for turning to this source is an apparently surprising concession made almost at the last moment. Retracting nothing from the ferocity of the denunciation of the author's main opponents, there occurs a gentler treatment of some different categories among the faithful.

> There are some doubting souls who need your pity. Others you should save by snatching them from the flames. For others your pity must be mixed with fear; hate the very clothing that is contaminated with sensuality (22–23).

It is a belated, but intelligible concession to the fact that not all forms of deviation from the norm belong to the same category, as Saint Paul had earlier indicated. In these matters sensitive judgement is absolutely unavoidable, and the necessity of differing responses calls for insight, wisdom, and compassion rather than the rhetoric of pollution, banishment, and exclusion.

My revisit to the twenty-five verses of the letter of Jude was intended to be a concrete reminder of the coexistence of traditions of exclusion and of inclusion from the very first formation of the institutional life of the Church. So much modern discussion of questions of power and authority has attempted to draw a discrete veil around, or to gloss, the severity of the biblical rhetoric against distortions of the faith, that I believe it necessary to start our treatment of this topic with an open recognition of this fact. Otherwise we shall conclude in one of the notable techniques for concealing the existence of real powers, namely the cloaking of them in the garments of "service." It is not, of course, that the idea of service is inherently corrupt. How could it be, for a Christian theologian, in the light of our Lord's words and example? The danger is rather that the mere invocation of service has become a way of evading the implications of a serious analysis of power. "Service," in a Christian theology of power and authority, is not corrupt; but it is corruptible, as we shall see.

The heritage of the documents of the Second Vatican Council on the matter of power and authority is complex, and has been analyzed many times. The relationship between the ecclesiology of the council and the Code of Canon Law adds further layers of complexity to the process of reception internal to the Roman Catholic Church. Those familiar with medieval and Tridentine Catholicism were thoroughly aware of the centuries-long discussion of *potestas ecclesiastica,* and of the definition in canon law of the separable but related powers of order and of jurisdiction.[4] The person who holds canonical power in its fullness has both the faculty of commanding that certain laws should be kept, and the institutional backing for enforcing these laws with appropriate sanctions if necessary. But it is the possession of a specific sacramental power which for the most part identifies which persons hold which jurisdictional powers. The concept of authority in the post-Tridentine period is almost completely dominated by the idea that specific people represent God vicariously in the exercise of church government. Although strictly speaking baptism is the sole, absolutely necessary sacrament for salvation and its administration is not restricted to the clergy, the fact that only those in Holy Orders have complete control over the eucharist and absolution gives them effective power over the degree to which ordinary Christians can participate in the means of grace.[5] The importance of this power is enhanced when one takes into account the damage inflicted by mortal sin after baptism, removable only by the effects of the further sacraments. In the medieval period, the use of this leverage in disputes with kingly power is absolutely overt, in theory and practice.

Dr. Guite invites us to compare a passage from *Lumen Gentium* with one from an encyclical of Leo XIII (*Satis Cognitum,* 1896). Speaking of the sending out of the Apostles by Christ, the Pope writes:

> Since this divine task was to last continually for ever, he attached to himself those who studied his teaching, and made them sharers in his power: and when he had called down the Spirit of truth from heaven upon them, he commanded them to traverse the world and to preach faithfully to all nations what he had taught and commanded them.[6]

The picture is of a jurisdictional power bestowed on the Apostles, as a result of which they have an entitlement to instruct the nations in obedience to the laws of the Church. By contrast, though the same phrase, "shares in his power" is used in *Lumen Gentium,* the context is different. Again speaking of the college of the twelve, with Peter at their head, it is said that the Lord sent them

> first of all to the children of Israel and then to all peoples (cf. Rom. 1:16), so that, sharing in his power, they might make all people his disciples, and sanctify and govern them (cf. Matt. 28:16–20; Mark 16:15; Luke 24:45–48; John 20:21–23) and thus spread the Church and, administering it under the guidance of the Lord, shepherd it all days until the end of the world (cf. Matt. 28:20).[7]

In this latter context "power" is less of a jurisdictional qualification, and more of a dynamic capacity by which the Apostles were enabled to propagate the Church by this mission.[8] This, and similar passages, constitute the "change of atmosphere" achieved by the Second Vatican Council, the prominent use of pastoral, moral, and spiritual categories to offset or supplement the more rigorously disciplinary motifs of the post-Tridentine era.

Eugenio Corecco has pointed out that the Second Vatican Council "chose to express itself, when dealing with the Church's power, by means of the unitary idea of *sacra potestas*."[9] This must be regarded as having a different character from that of the social power of the state; it is "identical with the binding salvic power inherent in word and sacrament," which together produces both the church and its social being (294). By contrast the Code of Canon Law only partially embodies the requisite change of perspective, and reintroduces a variety of *potestates: legislativa, executiva, iudicativa,* and *potestas interpretandi* (can. 129ff.), "unabashedly smacking of civil law" and the older theory of the *societas perfecta* (293).

Protestants, of course, tended to welcome the new "atmosphere" of the Second Vatican Council documents and to be anxious about the tendency of the Code. Still more have they come to mistrust the actual disciplinary measures recently taken against certain Roman Catholic theologians.[10] There is an understandable ecumenical concern that these proceedings embody a step backwards into an older, less congenial world of hierarchical authoritarianism. This unease is very widespread and all too readily poisons the "spiritual climate":[11] What is the point in the sophisticated work of the commissions on long-disputed theological doctrines, it is asked, if the machinery of church government is intent on handing down infallible pronouncements and on crushing dissent? But it is precisely this situation which needs more careful analysis, in the course of which it is advisable for us to remember the letter of Jude.

The Protestant reaction, in the first place, has to be related to both the European Reformation and the European Enlightenment. Concern about the exercise of power is explicitly articulated in the main Protestant confessional documents from the *Confessio Augustana* onwards.[12] But the interpretation of the sixteenth-century attempt made to distinguish between, and to separate, the spiritual and temporal "sword" and "authority" is anything but secure. Similarly unstable is the Enlightenment protest against "authoritarianism." Not merely are there limits to the practice of tolerance in civic societies (for example, the suppression of racial hatred), there is also the obvious phenomenon of liberal authoritarianism, the sometimes unconscious exercise of power to diminish or even eliminate the circulation of unfavored convictions. The legacy of both Reformation and Enlightenment actually requires an explicit treatment of the question of power in relation to the theology and life of the Church. In this matter one can by no means rely upon instinct and generalization, especially not when it comes to the examination of the powers of *episkope* or the episcopate.

Secondly, a shibboleth has been enunciated, which has achieved virtually canonical status, namely, "not power but service." Its source is supposed to be the dominical word and example. The exegesis, however, of the relevant texts (Mark 10:41–45; Matt. 20:20–28; Luke 22:24–30) is frequently faulty or partial. Jesus by no means denies the fact of inequality of power. There is to be rule in the Church; and such rule, by definition, carries the implication of the exercise of power. What is negated is the dominative exercise of power (the Greek term *katakurieuo* is used, Mark 10:42; 1 Pet. 5:3); what is affirmed is a power which serves.

But service, we have already noted, itself raises problems. Modern sociology encourages us to observe the fact of an instinct for the concealment of power, which is a virtually universal characteristic of all those upon whom powers are about to be bestowed. Inevitably it was on the lips of Mr. Tony Blair as he set off for Buckingham Palace to receive from the Queen the seals of his undeniably powerful office as Prime Minister of Great Britain and Northern Ireland; had he said, "I am about to become one of the most powerful people in the Western world," the public would have been confused and anxious. There is a collusive instinct among those with less power which confirms the propriety of this concealment, almost as though its public acknowledgment involved a kind of indecency. We are obscurely comforted by the illusion of equality. Yet the invocation of service need not involve hypocrisy. The use of the word itself, as we have said, is not inherently corrupt and corrupting. But it is plainly capable of being corrupted, both in the minds of those who hear it—if they interpret it to mean that the powerful person has, in reality, no power—and in the mind of those who use it—if they do so in order to conceal the reality of their power from their audience or from themselves.

But is the word "power" univocal in its use in public, political, or institutional contexts, and in theology and the church? It would undoubtedly be convenient if the concept of *sacra potestas* could be invoked to established a clear distinction between the life of the Church, and that of a state or institution. This is the nub of the issue, and at its heart lies the very mystery of salvation itself. For the incarnate word entered human history. But part of the garment of humility with which he clothed himself was the openness of his saving work to doubt and inquiry. The Gospels unhesitatingly affirm that from the first there were those who doubted; that is an inherent part of the case for their reliability. But we cannot have even a modest degree of confidence in the general historical veracity of the narratives without incurring the risks of critical inquiry.

What is true of the Word made flesh is *a fortiori* true of the Church. It too, in an analogous though different way, is located in time, human history, and culture.[13] It too is open to inquiry; and an integral part of confidence in the Church must be its willingness to be subject to historico-sociological analysis. That analysis neither proves, nor even adds to the faith claims made for its significance in God's plan of salvation. But because those claims relate to the historical experience of humankind, to concrete forms of slavery, sickness, and sin, they cannot assert a principled immunity from relevant forms of inquiry.

The contents of the letter of Jude are pertinent to this argument because it is a document revealing a community in the pangs of institutional creation. To avert one's eyes from the risks of that process is a serious mistake of judgment. The author is plainly threatened by the deviations he denounces; we have no way of deciding whether he is justified in his fears, or whether he is being unfair. In all probability he is conscious, like Saint Paul before him, of the weakness of his position, namely that he has no effective sanctions against his opponents. The enemy is within: "these people are a danger at your love feasts with their shameless carousings."[14] They are even spoken of as "shepherds."[15] Are they then already church leaders? If so, how could they be got rid of?

The importance of Jude, as of other documents of a similar period such as 1 and 2 Peter, is that it shows the agony and risk of the early communities in the face of dissent, disorder, and deviation. Idealizing accounts of the handing over of apostolic authority rarely mention this conflictual background. Some stress the unity and orderliness of the transition to episcopal oversight; others, with a different ecumenical agenda, tend to highlight the accommodating plurality of early modes of government. Both have vested interests in averting their eyes from the embarrassing rhetoric of Jude, because it sheds all too candid a light upon the struggle and risk entailed in the formation of church government.

But we know for certain that from the very first days of the Church there were those who abused their positions of power. Why else would the discreditable story of the disciples' dispute as to which of them should be greatest be remembered?[16] Why else would the author of 1 Peter warn the elders not to govern the flock for the sake of money or from a desire to dominate?[17] This biblical evidence of the existence from the first of the abuse of power justifies in itself the use both of a searching critique of the exercise of power in the Church and of institutional checks to avoid it.

Modern social sciences offer the Church very notable resources in this regard, and ecumenism would do well to take note of them. There are, of course, controversial features in the analysis of the distribution and exercise of power in the life of the Church from a sociological perspective. In the first place the concept of power, we soon discover, is itself unstable—or "essentially contested," as some have argued.[18] This means that theologians have to become involved in understanding the way in which "power" and "authority" have come to be understood in modern thought. It soon becomes apparent that the concept of "power" has attracted formidably negative connotations in the modern period, to such a degree that it seems to some to be unusable in relation to the institutional life of the Church. In this regard the open discussion of *potestas ecclesiastica* in medieval thought has a refreshing matter-of-factness about it. A church leader who fears a deviation in the community as much as did Jude, could well do with a law to appeal to, if for no other reason than to save the Church from arbitrary tyranny.

It is the modern social sciences which help us to identify what I consider to be a fact, namely that in the development of a canon of authoritative texts, together with a corps of authoritative interpreters, the Church incurred costs as well as benefits.[19] This development can, therefore, neither simply be legitimated as the will of God, nor be simply regretted as a decline from primitive standards of grace. It is a development in time and history, under the promised guidance of the Holy Spirit but attended with risks and temptations. The risks and temptations are apparent from the study of the history of the Church; they are also the daily currency of gossip and jokes. But they have yet to be spoken of with frankness and transparency in ecumenical texts, not least those dealing with the vexed subject of Authority in the Church.

The work of the Second Vatican Council in reminding the Roman Catholic Church of other themes in the rich stock of biblical and Catholic ecclesiology has been an essential part of the ecumenical movement of the last twenty-five years. The glorious opening words of *Lumen Gentium* remind us of the centrality of Christ and of the proclamation of the Gospel. The Church is first defined as a "sign and instrument . . . of communion with God and of unity among all,"[20] not as a juridical entity. It is, however, a visible organization in which "a divine and a human element" is brought together "in one complex reality."[21]

Provided that the reconciling and uniting inclusiveness of vision for the Church is first mentioned—the offer and reality of communion with God through the forgiveness of sin by grace alone—there should be no embarrassment about provision for discipline, including the sanction of exclusion. The point of a written code of law is not the subjugation of a people, but freedom from capricious exercises of power. Law, moreover, does not eliminate the necessity for wisdom and compassion. Many complex aspects of the life of the Church can be assisted by advice and counsel—the "doubting souls" who "need your pity." (Jude 22)—and do not belong to the realm of discipline at all. The function of law is to provide a publicly available and common standard of agreed procedures for the deciding of disciplinary matters, and the identification of those with the responsibility for decision, together with an account of the nature and boundaries of their competence. Law in the Church ought to be governed by theology which expounds the nature of the Church. But that theology is itself located in time and place by the unique and irreplaceable witness of the Scriptures. Theology is not a timeless and fixed corpus of material, but an ever renewed and renewing reflection upon a specific testimony in a specific context. This inherent dynamism constantly requires alertness, especially in the area of church law, to the necessity for change.[22]

The existence of disciplinary procedures is not, therefore, evidence of a debased or unspiritual understanding of the Church; nor is the exercise of discipline *ipso facto* a form of authoritarianism. The questions raised by recent events concern rather the competency of particular persons to make decisions, the content of these decisions, and the processes by which the decisions were arrived at.[23] The ecumenical significance of these events is considerable, but they are by no means unthinkable in a Protestant or Anglican context.[24] Certain responsibilities and powers are given to bishops in the Church of England by the Articles and the Ordinal, subject to the same limitations. Disciplinary actions are not, of themselves, unecumenical activities.

This paper has mainly been concerned with addressing the fact that the powers bestowed on particular people are accompanied by risks and temptations. There was a price to be paid in the development of authoritative church government. That Calvin and the church in Geneva paid this price (or rather we should say that the Anabaptists paid the price of the authoritative disciplinary procedures developed within Reformed ecclesiology) is as obvious a fact as, for example, that the early Church paid the price. The point I am making is of general application; in sociological theory, it is called, after Weber, the routinization of charisma.[25] The new churches and movements of our day constantly rediscover the difficulties of providing for a transmission of authority and for the regulation of the financial affairs of the Church. It is, in a certain way, a very obvious point to make; one might well think it so obvious that one would hardly devote a whole paper to it. But the fact is that it is virtually never mentioned in ecumenical documents.

But the doubt might well remain whether so vulgar and apparently secular a point *ought* to be made in a theological document. How is the process of institution building related to the discipline of a theological ecclesiology? There is a real danger that this point is never seriously tackled, neither by those who assert that Jesus instituted a college of Apostles, and after them calls a kind of standing committee of bishops to decide matters which the Apostles are not here to decide for themselves (as John Henry Newman once put it), nor by those who invoke the doctrine of the priesthood of all believers as an alternative version of the locus of decision-making authority. In neither case is the theological theory really sufficient to account for what actually happens when a rather large institution is faced with "certain individuals who have wormed their way in,"[26] to cite the letter of Jude.

Finally therefore we may consider as an example the course and conduct of an event such as this present meeting. In religious and theological intention we have met within the overarching context of God's love. We live in it, breathe in it, speak in it, think in it, puzzle and fret in it, disagree in it, but finally the psalmist is right when he said, "Yahweh's tenderness embraces all his creatures."[27] I want to speak of this as God's *energy,* in order to give it a different name than power; but the reasons are strategic rather than conceptual, so that we can identify the word when we hear it.

We might well, in an act of self-dedication, indeed of corporate dedication, have consciously dedicated ourselves at the start of this session to work within God's love. We might have said, "May the words of my mouth and the thoughts of our hearts be now and always acceptable to you, O Lord our energy and our Redeemer."[28]

But it would still remain the case that all participants in this meeting retain a variety of ordinary, created human powers. As the lecturer I have the power of giving or withholding an intention to be intelligible, audible, and even occasionally interesting. As an audience you have individually the power of your body language, the giving or withholding of signs of attentiveness (as Augustine pointed out—and things have not changed much over the centuries—yawning and looking at your watches are unmistakable signs of what's going on).[29] Those who chair a meeting have also certain powers in the event of misbehavior; they can quell disruptions; they can keep the speaker to time; they can do all in their power to keep the atmosphere focused and pleasant.

Now all these powers are the common levers to hand which we all enjoy in differing degrees within the conventions of a formal lecture. They apply to all kinds of meetings, not just to meetings assembled on the energy of God's love to advance the unity of God's Church. But they *do* apply to church meetings; and these powers may or may not be used so as to become part of, instruments in, the energy of God's love. And it is immediately obvious that there is no certainty that any given meeting, merely because it consciously or unconsciously intends to be within that energy, actually will conform to it.

If, however, we strenuously desire to do everything we can to ensure that God's energy fills our actions, that our powers remain open to the motivating and accompanying influence of God's energy, then common prudence suggests that we all learn some of the wisdom about the stray causes of irritation that arise: lecturers who bury their heads and fail to look at the audience, an audience which ostentatiously looks elsewhere, a chair who provokes tensions by failing to keep speakers to time. This wisdom relates to the wisdom of the Book of Proverbs within the canon of Holy Scripture. Here we find material borrowed from a plurality of sources, partially shaped and reshaped within Judaism, sometimes mentioning God, sometimes not, bearing on a variety of domestic and social situations, and an integral part of the disciplines of nurturing God's people. The kind of sociology of religion which, I believe, is helpful to the Church is not an omnivorous, omnicompetent, unchallengeable, and often unintelligible system of materialist concepts, but the accumulation of observations about what generally happens to religious groups of certain kinds, professing certain aims within particular contexts. The Church needs that wisdom if it is to use the ordinary, created powers of human beings gathered in institutions in such a way as to avoid the many temptations to the abuse of those same powers.

These powers do not simply reside with ordained people given particular offices and responsibilities. They also reside with a literate elite of scholars, and within representative lay people elected to serve on decision-making bodies. Responsible exercises of power and authority of all kinds require both spiritual self-awareness and self-discipline, reinforced by entering consciously into a tradition of wisdom. It also demands the creation of a climate of openness, and structures in which those with undoubted powers lay aside the mantel of invulnerability and allow those over whom they exercise power to speak frankly of their experience. In such a way, and perhaps only in such a way, will Christians come to live within the energy of God, which in Jesus Christ they know includes the essential experience of vulnerability.

Ecumenical theology has laid, I believe, the groundwork for confronting those questions. It is time to do so together and more openly.

Notes

1. For introduction to Jude, see R. J. Bauckham, *Jude, 2 Peter,* W.B.C. 50 (Waco, 1983), and Jonathan Knight, *2 Peter and Jude* (Sheffield, 1995).

2. W. G. Kümmel, *Introduction to the New Testament* (London, 1966), 59ff.

3. See R. E. Brown, *The Epistles of John* (London, 1993), 59ff.

4. At this point I should like to express my gratitude for, and dependence on the account given by Dr. Margaret Guite (née Hutchison) in her unpublished Ph.D. thesis, "Obedience as a Theme in the Documents of the Second Vatican Council" (University of Durham, 1980).

5. Hutchinson, 91.

6. *Satis Cognitum;* cited from *Acta Sanctae Sedis,* vol. 28 (1895–96), 717.

7. *Lumen Gentium,* §19.

8. Hutchison, 98.

9. "Aspects of the Reception of Vatican II in the Code of Canon Law," in G. Alberigo, J-P Jossua, and J. A. Komonchak, eds., *The Reception of Vatican II* (Washington, D.C., 1987), 288.

10. As described by T. F. Reece, *Inside the Vatican: The Politics and Organization of the Catholic Church* (Cambridge, Mass., 1996), 248–63.

11. See *The Ecumenical Directory.*

12. See CA XXVIII, *The Power of Bishops.*

13. *The Conference of Bishops of the Anglican Communion,* encyclical letter (1897): "A faith which is always or often attended by a secret fear that we dare not inquire lest inquiry should lead us to results inconsolent with what we believe, is already infected with a disease which may soon destroy it" (p. 20).

14. Jude 12; cf. 2 Pet. 2:13.

15. Jude 12. See also *Ascension of Isaiah* 3:21–31 from the early second century A.D.

16. Mark 9:33–37.

17. 1 Pet. 5:2.

18. See S. Lukes, ed., *Power* (Oxford, 1986), 8ff. For the idea of an "essentially contested concept," see W. B. Gallie, *Philosophy and the Historical Understanding* (London, 1964), 157–91.

19. See S. W. Sykes, "*Episcope* and Power in the Church," in B. D. Marshall, *Theology and Dialogue: Essays in Conversation with George Lindbeck* (Notre Dame, Ind., 1990), 191–212.

20. *Lumen Gentium,* §1.

21. Ibid., §8.

22. *Code of Canon Law, Latin-English Edition* (Washington, D.C., 1983), preface to the Latin edition, xx.

23. On this point, see Reece, *Inside the Vatican.*

24. The *Confessio Augustana,* for example, in its article on the power of bishops (Art. XXVIII), clearly states that

According to divine right, therefore, it is the office of the bishop to preach the Gospel, forgive sins, judge doctrine and condemn doctrine that is contrary to the Gospel, and exclude from the community the ungodly whose wicked conduct is manifest. All this is to be done not by human power but by God's Word alone. On this account parish ministers and churches are bound to be obedient to the bishops according to the saying of Christ in Luke 10:16, "He who hears you hears Me."

25. M. Weber, *Law in Economy and Society* (Cambridge, Mass., 1954).
26. Jude 4; cf. Gal. 2:4.
27. Ps. 145:9.
28. Ps. 19:12.
29. Augustine, *First Catechetical Instruction,* trans. J. P. Christopher (London, 1952), ch. 13, 19. "It often happens, too, that one who at first was listening gladly becomes exhausted either from listening or standing, and now opens his mouth no longer to assent, but to yawn, and even involuntarily gives signs that he wants to depart" (43–44).

www.ingramcontent.com/pod-product-compliance
Lightning Source LLC
Chambersburg PA
CBHW020354100426
42812CB00001B/56